The Mating Game

What Every Woman Should Know

by

Dr. Lyndon McGill

Sundial Press

Salem, Oregon USA

Published by
Sundial Press
2168 Lancaster Dr. N.E.
Salem, Oregon 97305

ISBN: 0-9631771-0-9
Library of Congress Catalog Number: 91-091486

1. Marriage.   2. Interpersonal relations.   3. Intimacy (Psychology)

Printed in the United States of America

10 9 8 7 6 5 4 3 2

Dedicated to:

Angie & Amber

Acknowledgements

Life is made rich by special individuals who assist us along the way. Unfortunately, many of these people do not receive the credit they deserve. I would like to take this opportunity to express my deepest gratitude to a few who have made significant contributions to this book as well as my life:

My staff, for their patience, understanding, and constructive criticism throughout the writing of this book.

My colleague and dear friend Dr. Coease Scott, who provided me with professional feedback and a clearer view of "the big picture."

My editors, Thorn and Ursula Bacon, for their professionalism and exceptional ability to bring this book to life.

My wife, Tami, for her love and devotion throughout a time-consuming project that often left her on her own.

My parents, Leroy and Hazel McGill, who provided me with a value system that has served me well, and whose 50-year marriage has shown me that commitment *can* last a lifetime.

Contents

Introduction

While our knowledge about love and relationships is at an all-time high, our success rate in these two vital areas is dismally low. Nearly half of all first marriages and two-thirds of second marriages fail. Especially distressing is the fact that the divorce rate among marriage counselors and psychotherapists is no less than that of the general public.

In the face of these staggering statistics, one can only conclude that much of the advice being peddled is ineffective. Although there is some helpful information available that offers a variety of problem-solving solutions for a number of couples, marriage continues to be an unstable institution, and countless lives are disrupted and shattered every day because of separation and divorce.

Concerned by these facts, and aware of the devastating effects domestic turmoil is having on the lives and health of many of my patients, I embarked upon a quest to discover the fundamental cause of conflict between men and women. Since the problems preceding the breakup of most relationships are all too common, I was convinced that something consistent must be taking place.

Through research, counseling, participation in various support groups, personal experiences, and conducting *The Mating Game Seminars*, I have discovered some fascinating aspects of human behavior that largely determine the longevity of a male-female relationship, as well as the general health of the individuals involved.

Men and women don't seem to have much trouble getting together—as my grandmother used to say, "There's a lid for every pot"—but they do have a lot of trouble staying together (keeping the lid on the pot).

The crux of the problem in the male-female dynamic lies not in the incompatibility of the bodies but in the incompatibility of the minds. While bodies may remain in a relationship, the minds are often elsewhere. But the body eventually follows the mind to maintain a sense of connectedness.

The secret to success in the mating game is not how to *get* a man interested in you, it's how to *keep* him interested. Love does pretty well on its own until life gets in the way. Then, a blissful marital heaven can quickly turn into a fiery hell.

Why do two people who love each other inflict such misery upon themselves and those around them? What is the common denominator that drives a couple apart? What prevents deterioration of a "good thing?" How can the fun be put back into the mating game to make it an enjoyable and rewarding experience for both players? The answers to these questions can be found in the chapters ahead.

Too many men and women are playing the mating game with little formal training in matters of love and the care and maintenance of a healthy relationship. Marriage for these people too often turns out to be a double-blind study that fails; unfortunately, society pays for the experiment.

Perhaps we should first license people to engage in the mating game, instead of thrusting them together and *then* giving them the license. It's a sorry state of affairs when we are more skilled at running machines than our own lives.

Dissension between the sexes is a vicious circle. Children growing up in a dysfunctional household where respect is lacking and relationships are strained tend to follow in their parent's footsteps. Statistics show that abused children are four times more likely to become abusive mates and parents. Adults must learn better relationship skills in order to provide a harmonious setting for their offspring, as well as for themselves. It is just as easy for children to follow the example of a healthy pattern of living as it is to adapt to a violent and destructive lifestyle.

Our society emphasizes the singular instead of the plural. We promote the self instead of the whole, and we reward superiority instead of uniqueness. By failing to divide the responsibility among several players and fostering teamwork, we place it all upon the individual, forcing him to be highly competitive and even distrustful. This sets him up for deep anxiety and, ultimately, despair when his expectations are not met. Unfortunately, this paradigm has filtered into our personal relationships.

We have focused on materialism and self-aggrandizement so much that we have failed to perfect our people skills and the art of being cooperative and flexible. As a result, we are long on expectations and short on patience and empathy. Caring and sharing are rare commodities.

Life has become a paradox. Dwelling in apartments, town houses, and zero-lot-line homes we now live closer to each other than we ever have, but we know each other less. In fact, we often feel a stronger bond to those we *don't* live with—respecting more those whom we know less.

While the media keeps on painting a cornucopia of life and love with make-believe Hollywood crayons, the public is becoming disillusioned from consistently encountering unmet expectations. The elite continue to rob the masses to finance their dreams, and the gap between poverty and affluence widens. This creates a fragmented society that has little respect for itself and, consequently, becomes a breeding ground for social ills.

There is no doubt that the twenty-first century will belong to responsible and accountable individuals—those who are willing and able to take charge of their own health and happiness, which includes forming strong, supportive relationships. Despite sporadic successes and a few notable achievements, our economic, health care, educational, political, social, and judicial systems have failed to provide us with the security they inferred. Now we must roll up our sleeves and go to work ourselves, rebuilding our lives upon a solid foundation of truth and morality. Since abandoning these principles did not work, let's try it again *with* them.

You will discover that I have devoted as much of this book to the *facts of life* as I have to the *birds and the bees*. There's a reason for that. Most problems encountered in love are due to misunderstandings about life. We fail at life and then take it out on love. But as we begin to understand more about life, we automatically become more successful at love. And by looking into the inner sanctum of the human spirit, discovering who we are, who our partners are, and what we both want out of life, we become experts at the mating game.

Contrary to what we have been told, ignorance is not bliss. It's suicide. With the emergence of AIDS, forming and maintaining a strong, monogamous relationship has become a matter of life and death. We can no longer take the mating game for granted. We must become knowledgeable in matters of the heart to extend our lives and increase our happiness.

This work deals exclusively with heterosexual relationships. Although some suggestions may be applicable to all relationships, the heterosexual dynamic presents some unique problems that require special solutions. As we sometimes discover, there are exceptions to the rule, and this book is by no means exempt from such. But since most failing male-female relationships share a common pathway, my generalizations will be helpful to most couples.

This is not a book of quick fixes nor a set of rules to be followed implicitly. You will simply be provided with a new perspective that will allow you to write your own game plan for life and love.

This work is not intended to be a substitute for professional counseling or therapy, since some dilemmas require specialized help. Still, you can do a lot to heal your own relationship when you are provided with the proper tools and adequate knowledge.

Some case studies presented in this book are composites, and in every instance the names and identifying details have been altered to preserve confidentiality. I thank those whose struggles with the mating game contributed to the conception of this book, for without their labor and suffering it would not have been born. It is because of them that I have come to understand why each gender has its own set of rules and responsibilities, which, if adhered to, ultimately unite and empower us all; and why, when we disregard these boundaries and attempt to cross over, we inevitably fall into the narrow yet deep abyss that separates us.

The Predicament

1

𝒩othing has had, or will ever have, more of an effect on the course of humanity than the interaction between men and women. Wars have been started, fought, even won or lost, as a result of the forces generated by the male-female dynamic, and it is likely that scores of potential conflicts have been averted by its powers as well. Besides shaping our history, the mating game is influencing our lifestyle and leaving its mark on our music, literature, art, science, and our economy—in fact, almost every aspect of our lives is affected by the success or failure of relationships involving men and women.

Looking back, the most significant change in the game occurred with the arrival of the Industrial Age when women moved into the work force and subsequently became liberated. With this dramatic change came an increase in the level of tension between the sexes. Today, the male-female dynamic has become a primary socioeconomic problem and the effects are reverberating into literally every aspect of life on this planet.

The next most significant change was the invention of the birth control pill and other effective means of contraception. Women were no longer confined to a life of perpetual pregnancy and child care, and were free to compete with men on a more equal basis. Though many forms of contraception have side effects, women have readily adopted them for their emancipation value.

The traditional family with its time-honored roles has been undergoing some drastic changes. Whether these changes will ultimately prove to be beneficial remains to be seen, but it is obvious that they cannot occur without considerable cost to humanity, both in lives and relationships.

Although the figures vary, most current studies show that despite the advances made by the sexual revolution and women's liberation, many people are dissatisfied with some aspect of their relationships with the opposite sex. A significant number of women are fed up with men and openly express their increasing frustration and disillusionment. Men express their dissatisfaction as well, and quickly point to the women as the source of the problem. But women are more disappointed than men. A Glamour magazine poll found that 77 percent of the men surveyed would marry the same person again, but only 50 percent of the women would do so. According to the Gallup Group, 50 percent of men believe that it is better to go through life married instead of single, but only 37 percent of women agree.

Scores of self-help books and articles on relationships promote a *find-out-what-type-of-person-you-got-stuck-with* methodology. Unfortunately, this labeling diminishes the mutual respect between the sexes and causes them to look at each other with a jaundiced eye. Ending a relationship becomes much easier and can be rationalized when a partner fits a particular problem category.

In their bid for equality, women may have lost as much as they have gained. Besides the threat of competition, men with working wives enjoy a higher standard of living, yet they fail to do their equal share of the housework. This leaves women tired and resentful, especially when they realize that their salaries go to finance larger "toys" for the "boys." Perhaps it is the male, after all, who has gained the most from women's liberation and is now capitalizing on the female's willingness to sacrifice herself and her time to improve his status in life. And, with women in the work force, men don't have to wait until five o'clock to womanize.

Though there is evidence that working women suffer less depression than housewives, career women do pay a price. An evaluation of 123 women who graduated from business schools in 1977 and 1978 revealed they were suffering significantly more stress than their male counterparts. Other studies have shown that women's physical health has deteriorated relative to men's over the last 25 to 30 years. Respiratory ailments, ulcers, and infertility among women have risen sharply. Working women are more likely to be alcoholics than are housewives. Contrary to the notion that most women enjoy having a career, an A.C. Nielsen survey found that only 19 percent of working women hold down a job because they want to. Most women have joined the work force because they or their families need the money.

Men married to working women also show signs of strain. A recent study found such men to be less satisfied with both their work and lives in general than husbands whose wives stayed home. Many of these men were worriers, fretting over their health, their jobs, and their relationships.

Considering the amount of conflict, one might wonder why men and women still have anything to do with each other. As philosopher Alan W. Watts describes it, "We fall in love with people and possessions only to be tortured by anxiety for them."

Obviously, perpetuation of our species is dependent

upon male-female sexual interaction. But beyond that, living with a member of the opposite sex is known to promote health and longevity. The National Center for Health Statistics reports that divorced people—both male and female—get sick more often, sustain more injuries, and die earlier than those who stay married. Divorced people have higher death rates from heart disease, cancer, pneumonia, high blood pressure, and liver cirrhosis.

According to researchers at the University of California at San Francisco, men between the ages of forty-five and sixty-four who live without a spouse are twice as likely to die within ten years as are those of the same age group who are married. Other studies have shown that rates of smoking and drinking are higher among single people. With a University of Michigan study showing that married men earn an average of 26 percent more than single men, it literally pays to form a strong relationship with a member of the opposite sex. We therefore find ourselves in a predicament: *we can neither live with each other nor without each other*.

When evolutionary processes hit a dead end, a new direction often presents itself that increases the chances of survival of the species. Perhaps evidence of this phenomenon in our current socioevolutionary process is the recent trend back to traditional family roles and values for a more stable family environment. AIDS, drug abuse and rising violence are undoubtedly fueling this change. But even beyond that, there is a hint of nostalgia and a touch of wistfulness in the hearts and minds of men and women as they attempt to turn back the clock to the Good Old Days. Music and fashions from the past are popular again. More and more movies focus on historical periods, and advertising is turning away from futuristic themes to traditional ones. A men's movement attempting to reclaim masculinity is gaining attention. A growing number of people are pining for the time when men were "men" and women were "women," though we debate what that really means.

In many of our attempts to improve upon nature we have consistently come full circle. This is not to depreciate the great discoveries and inventions that have truly benefitted humanity, but we have often tried to improve particular aspects of our world only to find that altering nature ultimately created a greater threat to our existence. To satisfy our desire for convenience we industrialized the world and developed modes of transportation that ultimately polluted the planet. Herbicides, pesticides, artificial colors and preservatives may have enhanced the looks and life span of our foods, but they also have caused serious health problems. Some medicines and vaccines developed to cure our ills have turned on us, and the healing powers of herbs are appreciated once again. Natural childbirth is in vogue, and to reclaim the ozone layer we are discarding aerosols and going back to pump and spritz.

Altering nature creates a greater threat to our existence. Perhaps this is also true in the mating game. But can we go back to traditional roles at this point? Economics say no. Therefore, we must be creative in our approach to attain sound relationships and come up with a plan that cooperates with our nature instead of conflicts with it.

Whether we evolved over millions of years or were created by God and placed in the Garden of Eden, men and women have played specific roles that have changed very little until recently. David Barash, in his excellent treatise *The Hare And The Tortoise*, clearly delineates the problems we are currently experiencing as a result of the immense gap between our biology (tortoise) and our sociology (hare): our nature and our nurture. In essence we are making great demands on ourselves through our complex societies, but our biology remains too primitive to keep up.

In the early days, males and females had clearly defined roles. Men were the hunters and protectors, women were the camp tenders and nurturers. As time passed, these roles began to blur and overlap. Although the game changed (sociology), the players (biology) did not, and we became a confused and anxious species. This schism is the very root of the conflict between men and women, and destroys countless lives.

Studies have shown that all-male gatherings tend to become aggressive, while all-female groups generally form stronger relationships and verbalize more. Mixing men and women leads to sexual relationships.

These innate behavioral tendencies can be attributed to the interaction of primitive males and females. During the hunt, males found it necessary to cooperate with family and friends, but contact with outside males fostered competition and aggression. Since females posed little competitive threat and, instead, represented new sexual prospects, male aggressiveness toward females was never a major issue and escaped genetic imprinting. Although outside females may have posed a competitive threat to the other females, the feminine sense of family and nurturing was an overriding factor. Males engaging in the hunt had to keep communication to a minimum to avoid alerting their prey. Females, on the other hand, were encouraged by their environment to communicate and cooperate.

Now that women compete with men in the workplace, men's basic role as the provider is compromised. Although society accepts women in the work force, men's biology does not. Consequently, the tension level between men and women has risen several notches.

Men and women don't seem to have much trouble falling in love, they just have trouble *staying* in love. Somewhere along the line behavior turns negative, misunderstandings rise to the surface, and the relationship deteriorates. Besides infidelity, the reason many women file for divorce is their mate's unreasonable behavior. Why do men often become moody and withdrawn shortly after marriage or cohabitation? What triggers this behavioral change?

Men and women are a lot more alike than we have been led to believe, but the emphasis each gender places on various aspects of their lives varies to a significant degree. When these emphases clash, there is trouble in paradise. Let's take a look.

The Nature Of The Game

2

$\mathcal{A}$ll humans and animals are motivated by the same basic urges I call The Four "F"s: *fight, flight, feed,* and *fuck.* Although my use of the word *fuck* for the copulatory urge may be offensive to some, it does start with the letter "F," and it certainly relays the basic concept of this proclivity.

Aside from inadvertent or abnormal fluctuations in hormones or brain neurotransmitter substances, practically all human and animal behavior can be ascribed to one or more of these basic urges. To think we are more complex and operate independently of them is a foolish assumption. And the first step toward understanding ourselves, as well as the opposite sex, is acknowledging the power of these urges. By acknowledging these proclivities and identifying instances in which we cannot express them in a normal fashion (repression/denial), we will discover the root of the conflict between men and women, and most of our other social ills.

When we encounter a situation or stimulus, our nervous system, via the five senses, takes in information and transmits it to the brain for classification: positive or negative, harmful or safe, pleasurable or painful. The brain's final decision determines our subsequent behavior. The following diagram depicts this process:

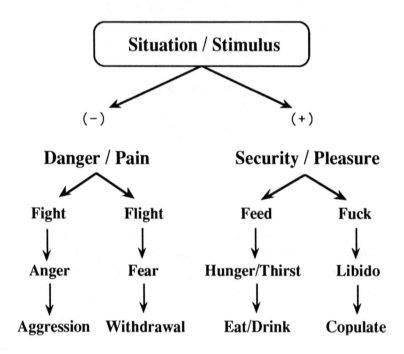

It's not too difficult to categorize animal behavior according to the four basic urges, since most animals live fairly simple lives. Humans, on the other hand, live complicated lives and our behavior is a little more complex—often the by-product of a combination of urges. Still, most of our actions can be attributed to a predominant urge, and it will help to classify them for the sake of discussion. Here is a partial list:

Primary Urges

Fight	Flight	Feed	Fuck
Aggression	Fleeing	Eating	Procreation
Anger	Withdrawal	Drinking	Sexual Pleasure
Hostility	Insecurity	Elimination	Appearance
Protection	Shyness	Socializing	Grooming
Work/Sports	Avoidance	Relaxing	Bonding
Competition	Anxiety	Companionship	
Authority	Fears/Phobias	Home(ing)	
Rank	Superstitions	Security	
Fatherhood	Huddling	Dependence	
Male Bonding	Bonding	Female Bonding	
Crusades	Inhibitions	Nurturing	
Conquest		Motherhood	
Heroism		Non-Sexual Affection	
Possessiveness		Compassion	
Assertiveness			
Defensiveness			
Discipline			

Higher Human Urges

Inquisitiveness
Playfulness
Laughter
Weeping
Creativity
Spirituality
Meditation

Few areas of science are as littered with contradictory "research" as the study of the differences between the sexes. Yet experts agree that males and females alike operate under the influence of the basic urges.

Common human behaviors can be attributed to the Four "F"s, which constitute our *basic* reality, while our higher aspirations can be attributed to the *higher* human urges. As you can see, most of our time here on earth is spent trying to satisfy the *basic* urges.

Various personality types are related to a dominance of a particular urge. These traits also correspond with Hippocrates' four temperaments: *choleric, melancholy, phlegmatic,* and *sanguine.*

Fight (Choleric): **Extroverted, aggressive, controlling, possessive**
Flight (Melancholic): **Inhibited, nervous, skeptical, insecure**
Feed (Phlegmatic): **Quiet, laid-back, flexible, yet dependent**
Fuck (Sanguine): **Sexy, flirtatious, talkative, narcissistic, phony**

We are born with a general dominance of a particular urge, giving us our basic personality trait. These traits intensify when we are under stress, confirming that they are defense mechanisms, reinforced from an early age. These traits determine, to a great extent, the dynamics of a relationship. Fight-dominant people are controllers; flight-dominant ones, distancers; feed-dominant ones, clingers; and fuck-dominant ones, self-centered.

As the emphasis on a particular urge changes, so do personality and behavior. And by creating anxiety in a less dominant urge, personality and behavior can be temporarily altered. More on this later.

Our basic urges originate in the primitive or lower centers of our brains. Brain researcher Dr. Paul MacLean maintains that we have three separate, yet interconnected, brain levels. The first and lowest center is considered the reptilian brain. This center is responsible for our hunting, fighting, establishing territory, homing, feeding, and mating activities. The second level, the limbic system, or what Dr. MacLean calls the paleomammalian brain, deals with the emotions that guide behavior. The third and highest level, the cortex, is the human advantage—although sometimes disposed to exploitation and subversion.

The first two levels, the reptilian and limbic systems, are common to both humans and animals. But the cortex is more developed in humans and allows us to remember, to reason, to solve problems, to speak, to anticipate, to expect, to plan, to complicate our lives, to hold grudges, and to forgive. It allows us to simultaneously create a world filled with endless opportunities and encumbrances. It also shuttles us emotionally between heaven and hell at supersonic speeds.

When we analyze human behavior we find that the cortex mainly serves to compound actions stemming from basic urges. Although we see the complex versions turned out by the cortex, the underlying motivators are usually *fight, flight, feed,* and *fuck.* Our cortex has merely allowed us to complicate our lives and the world to such an extent that we have lost sight of our basic needs and motives. To get to the root of our behavioral problems—including the dissension between the sexes—and to formulate solutions, we must take a closer look at our basic urges.

Basic Urges

(Autonomic Nervous System)

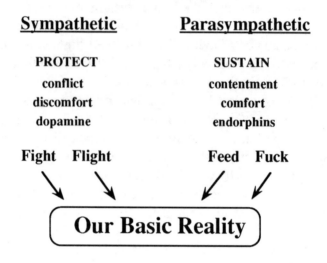

Our behavior and many of our bodily functions are under the control of the autonomic nervous system, which strives to keep the body's internal environment stable. The autonomic nervous system has two divisions: *sympathetic* and *parasympathetic*. The sympathetic division is our built-in alarm and defense system. It controls the body's ability to meet threats through the fight or flight mechanisms.

The parasympathetic division, on the other hand, is our maintenance system, controlling the vegetative functions, such as digestion (feed) and sexual arousal (fuck). The parasympathetic system replenishes energy stores and renews us. Put simply, the sympathetics bring us discomfort and the parasympathetics bring us comfort.

The sympathetics and parasympathetics normally act in a balanced reciprocal fashion. For example, when we become angry (fight) or anxious (flight), the increased sympathetic stimulation causes digestion (feed) to slow due to the reciprocal inhibition of the parasympathetics. This, in turn, causes our appetite to diminish and we say that we are *too upset to eat.* That's why workaholics (fight) often skip lunch, or supper, or breakfast. Moreover, food already in the system may not digest properly and indigestion results. When one system consistently outweighs the other, such as with the high levels of anxiety created by our stressful world (sympathetic dominance), mental and physical illness occurs, as well as behavioral problems. Normal responses get fouled up and we act conversely. We overeat when we aren't hungry, we drink when we're not thirsty, and we have sex when we really don't need to.

An important function of the sympathetic system is to release the hormone adrenaline (epinephrine). When we encounter a real or perceived threat, the sympathetic nervous system prepares us to fight or take flight, depending upon whether our senses tell us we can overcome the situation or we are likely to be harmed by it.

If we decide to stay and fight, the sympathetics prepare us for battle by shunting blood to the upper half of our body, especially to the muscles of the chest and arms to improve strength and endurance. That's why our face turns red and we feel tense in our upper body when we are angry (fight urge). If we decide to run (flight), the sympathetics shunt blood to the lower half of our body, especially to the leg muscles, so they can carry us away from the danger. That's why our face often turns white when we're frightened: blood drains from the head to the lower body. In both instances the pupils dilate to improve vision.

There are times when the fight/flight urges conflict with each other and we become *too scared to move*, unable to react. Until one force wins out over the other, we remain frozen and indecisive.

Observation of bodily reactions can be a valuable tool in assessing response to a given situation. It can allow you a short time to prepare for or avert negative behavior before it occurs. Unfortunately, humans are not as perceptive of these signals as are animals.

Close evaluation of the Four "F"s reveals that men and women emphasize different urges. Women place greater value on relationships and cooperation, while men revere work, competition, and sex. Women are motivated more by the *feed* urge, while men tend to be motivated by the *fight* and *fuck* urges. Many women also value their work, but it usually is not their primary focus in life.

Basic Urges
(Autonomic Nervous System)

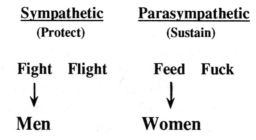

Men have an innate desire to be powerful and successful (fight). This stems from their classic role as the provider for the family. Warren Farrell, Ph.D., author of *Why Men Are The Way They Are*, says that men's primary fantasy is sex and their secondary fantasy is being successful or hero-figures, which increases their chances of having sex with a greater quantity and higher quality of females. This explains why research has found that males between the ages of 12 and 40 think about sex an average of six times an hour, and why their dreams are often of a sexual nature.

A woman's primary fantasy is mating with a successful

male, says Farrell. Her secondary fantasy is her appearance, since beauty increases her chances of attracting a more powerful and successful male. Farrell points out that the best selling men's magazines are *Playboy* and *Sports Illustrated*, while the best selling women's magazines are *Better Homes and Gardens* and *Cosmopolitan*. Men enter a relationship for validation through beauty and sex, while women do so for security and the family/home concept. The contrast in the graphics of these magazines alone confirms the behavioral differences in men and women.

Farrell's theory is supported by several other experts. According to a five-year study by the International Mate Selection Project, directed by David M. Buss of the University of Michigan, which involved 50 scientists, 37 cultures in 33 countries, and more than 10,000 people of both sexes:

"Men worldwide place greater value on mates who are young and physically attractive. Women prefer mates who are ambitious and industrious...Animal studies have confirmed the theory that females prefer mates who bear greater gifts, hold better territories or display higher rank."

According to Jeffrey Ullman, author of *The Singles Almanac,* men are more concerned about a woman's looks than who she is. Women also admire good-looking men, but they place more emphasis on intelligence, power, competence, and confidence.

Dr. Joyce Brothers says that men fall in love faster than women, usually deciding within seven seconds whether or not they want to know a woman better. Women are more concerned with how much money a man makes, which can take a little longer to ascertain. No wonder money is the best face-lift a man can buy!

A man's identity is rooted in work and sex, while a woman's is rooted in her appearance and relationships. By adding a few other items we can construct a list of areas in which men and women are most likely to suffer anxiety and identity crises.

Identity

Males	Females
Work	Appearance
Sex	Relationships
Sports	Home
Possessions	Children

Male suicide is usually tied to a career failure, while female suicide is often the result of a failed relationship. Men are more envious of wealth and fame; women are more envious of beauty and friendship. According to Dr. Brothers, "Male jealousy is more possessive and has a large sexual component." Female jealousy consists largely of "a fear of being replaced."

Typical male behaviors fall under the sympathetic division of the autonomic nervous system, while female behaviors favor the parasympathetic side. With compassion and nurturing falling into the feed/parasympathetic category, this helps to explain why men are generally not as sympathetic toward an ill partner as are women. This stems from the fact that men have been conditioned over the years to be the providers and protectors, emphasizing the fight/sympathetic urge, while women have traditionally been the nurturers and comforters.

There are other differences between men and women that cause misunderstanding and conflict. Acknowledging these differences leads to more empathy and respect, which leads to better relationships and more fun in the mating game. Let's take a closer look.

Through The Looking Glass

3

$\mathcal{D}$uring early fetal development (fifth to sixth week) the male embryo, at the direction of the Y-chromosome, normally gets a shot of androgen hormones. This causes it to begin differentiating into a male. Until this event, male and female fetuses are relatively the same.

Five months after conception the female embryo is about two weeks ahead of the male in development. At birth, she is about four weeks ahead. She walks and talks earlier, and enters puberty about two to three years earlier.

Women live longer than men; men are more apt to fight and kill each other. Men, as well as the males of most animal species, tend to be more aggressive and active. Men generally have better spatial abilities (reading maps and figuring out mazes), while women are better at verbal tasks and learning foreign languages. Men experience a higher incidence of speech and reading problems, and more men than women are left-handed. Men have better day vision; women, night vision. Women are more sensitive to touch, taste, smell, and hearing, and they generally have better manual dexterity and fine coordination. Women sing on key more frequently than men do. Females appear to be more interested in those around them. Women dream about friendly interactions with other women; men dream about other men and confrontations with strangers. When men dream about women, it usually involves sex. Women don't dream as much about sex.

Some of these differences may be explained by the tendency for each sex to rely more on one side of the brain: females, the left hemisphere; males, the right hemisphere. Research has shown that each half of the brain is assigned certain tasks, and females have a greater ability to integrate both sides due to having about 40 percent more neurons in the corpus callosum, the nerve network connecting the two hemispheres. Some experts feel this helps to explain *women's intuition*.

Left Brain	Right Brain
Language	Visual-spatial
Reasoning	Intuition
Logic	Spontaneous
Detail-oriented	Holistic
Disciplined	Emotional
	Artistic
	Imaginative
	Musical
	Sexual

Music has been an integral component of all cultures and is characteristic of the era. It plays a significant role in the mating game, and its selection or performance often reflects the mental state of the listener or performer. Since music is predominately a right-brain function, it is logical that it would be used to set a mood. With movement (visual-spatial) and light (visual) also being right-brain stimulants, it is easy to explain the current use of flashing lights and exaggerated body movements by performers in their attempts to motivate and impress an audience. Movements executed during dancing are attempts to draw attention. Animals also dance and move about in peculiar ways to make sure they are noticed.

The right brain highly influences sexual performance. This further explains the concomitant use of music with courting and sexual activities. With males lateralizing more to the right hemisphere, this may help to explain why men are more sexually active than females and usually don't like to talk (left hemisphere) while having intercourse. Talking requires mobilization of the left brain and hampers the ability to fantasize and concentrate on sexual matters.

Victims of a stroke on the left side of the brain that impairs the language center may still be able to swear. Since swear words are more emotional, they have a better chance of being accepted and retained by the right brain. This explains why some individuals eschew normal conversation during sex, yet get turned on by swear words uttered by their partner.

Many couples engage in passionate lovemaking following a fight or argument. Since the emotions associated with a dispute are significantly influenced by the right brain, as is sexual activity, a common pathway may mix and augment these behaviors. Perhaps the thin line between love and hate is made up of only a few neurons.

Even during bouts of sickness, many males desire sex and almost consider it medicinal. History supports the idea that sexual activity has somewhat of a curative effect on various ailments—at least in the male—since a variety of literary works mention females lying with ill males to nurse them back to health.

Some of our frustration with the opposite sex starts at an early age. Girls advance and mature faster than boys. Being aggressive and competitive, some males lose their self-image and suffer inferiority complexes when female classmates outdo them. Conversely, some females at this point develop a superiority complex, deeming males slow and retarded. Having to compete academically, boys and girls are alienated, yet true to nature they remain attracted to each other. This love-hate dynamic creates an element of uncertainty, and the anxiety level of male-female interaction rises.

Perhaps this is why females usually date males a few years their senior: an attempt to associate with boys who are on a more equitable intellectual plane, and to escape the immaturity of their male classmates. Many females form a relationship with a male who is older and higher on the security scale—representing a rescuer/hero or father figure (good provider). While this may be nature's plan, it reinforces women's dependency on men.

The heterosexual mating process escalates dramatically during the adolescent years. According to a recent survey conducted by the Centers for Disease Control, more than half of all American high school teen-agers have had sex (61 percent of boys and 48 percent of girls).

The human mating game resembles that of the animal world and has remained unchanged through the ages. Here is a brief outline of the stages:

1. Personal grooming by both sexes to maximize visual and olfactory (smell) appeal; utilization of verbal (left-brain) appeal—paying compliments, making promises, giving sympathy, etc.

2. Interaction or cruising, either in groups or one-on-one.

3. Male is attracted visually, and eventually by smell and intonation, to a particular female.

4. Male usually initiates the courting phase through verbal and physical gestures.

5. Female either accepts or rejects the male. (It is interesting to note that most males are less dissuaded by verbal rejection than by physical signs of such.)

6. Pair formation eventually occurs and courting increases.

7. Marriage or cohabitation.

8. Copulation (Note: #7 and #8 are often reversed).

The first interaction of a mating nature, in most cases, occurs during the adolescent years. Same-sex groups form in an apparent spirit of camaraderie, which represents security or strength in numbers, and then these groups interact in a display-and-survey manner. Both sexes are well-groomed to maximize their attractiveness, and ready to meet thc candidates.

As interaction progresses, pair-formation takes place— usually initiated by the male and ultimately affirmed by the female—and courting increases. When a male is rejected by a particular female, he usually moves on to another prospect—someone, perhaps, who is a little lower on his scale of expectations. If he is set on having a particular female, however, he may be persistent in his efforts to entice her, and his methods may become creative and extravagant. Most males prefer an element of resistance on the part of the female, which increases the value of the conquest.

Utilization of various material goods has long been a part of the human courting repertoire. Some items enhance one's own appeal, others bring favors or obligate to some degree. Fine clothing and jewelry attract attention and signify or insinuate social and/or financial status. Men usually adorn themselves in a way that projects power or success to attract more, better-looking women. Women dress to accentuate their appearance or sexual appeal to attract a more powerful, successful man. Although some women enjoy a *quantity* of suitors, most are concerned about the *quality* of an exclusive man.

Most men believe strongly in the aphrodisiacal power of material assets and use them to compensate for feelings of inadequacy. Expensive homes, condos, automobiles, boats, airplanes, etc., augment or compensate for attractiveness and serve to daunt the competition. With the female's migration into the workplace and her accessibility to a similar standard of living and the same symbols of success, male frustration and anxiety have substantially increased. When a woman outdoes a man in one department, he will often look for another way to impress her. If such an effort becomes too great, he may move on to a more impressionable female.

Men receive validation through their ability to protect and provide. When these attributes are no longer necessary or appreciated, men lose their self-esteem and become angry and frustrated. If their anger and frustration continue for an extended period, apathy sets in. But put such a man in touch with a woman who needs and appreciates what he has to offer and watch him come alive!

Attractive people usually have an ample supply of suitors. But once the initial mating phase is over and the partners get to know one another, factors other than outward appearance determine the longevity of the relationship. Although attractive individuals may be at an initial advantage in the mating game, the success of their pair-formation is ultimately dependent upon the same considerations as works for the rest of us: satisfaction of our basic urges. Attractive people experience additional problems, such as increased jealousy and competition, higher levels of expectation, and more difficulty accepting the aging process.

Some not-so-attractive people maintain a respectable number of opposite-sex acquaintances. Observation of these individuals reveals that they make the most of their personality and body language, and they are generally self-confident and not too self-conscious. They are adept at instilling excitement and vitality into their relationships, and being around them is a positive and uplifting experience. Their secret is that they can maintain a good self-image without having to depend solely upon others for validation.

Due to the male's biological tendency to pursue and be aggressive, his assuming the role of the *initiator* in the mating game is appropriate. While some men prefer an aggressive female, this is not consistent with innate male tendencies. Most men feel threatened by an overbearing female and recoil from her once the intrigue of the role reversal has worn off. Besides, some aggressive females eventually get tired of their role and long to be pursued.

Since females exhibit a greater ability to sit still, they make better *receptors*, observing various males' courting behavior and ultimately deciding with whom to mate. Less-desirable females have to augment their mating value in some way and put forth more effort to be noticed.

The acceptance or rejection option exercised by the female in the formation of a relationship is the first important determinant in the mating game. She decides with whom she will mate, and this puts the quality of the breeding potential under her control. The male, on the other hand, breeds with practically any available female. This is nature's way of dividing up the responsibilities of perpetuating the species: the female concentrates on quality; the male on quantity. The males pursue, the females resist. This is typical male and female mating behavior.

Observation of couples passing on the street reveals the subtle power of our specific proclivities. If it is not a threatening situation, and the couples do not know each other, the males will invariably look at the passing female, while the females look at each other. The men are sizing up the women for sexual potential; the women are sizing up their competition. Proof again that men focus on sex, and women on beauty.

Until sufficient change occurs in the basic nature of males and females and their respective sense of self, the most stable domestic setting will be the one in which the male is the provider and protector, and the female is the mother and nurturer. Although a few males make attempts to assume some of the female's traditional responsibilities, they usually do so unsuccessfully. More cooperation and sharing of responsibility is needed from both sides, but to alter our time-honored roles is to go against our very nature. And changing the basic nature of men and women will take a few more million years.

Some "experts" condemn traditional gender stereotyping and recommend a role reversal. Yet, the domestic upheaval and ensuing effects on our society from altering the status quo shows that this social evolution cannot take place without substantial cost to humanity. The question is whether it is worth the cost; and if so, how many individuals are willing to sacrifice their children, their relationships, and themselves in this effort to "advance" humankind?

The Repression Progression

4

*L*ike most animals, we are endowed with the need to express our basic urges in healthy ways and in adequate amounts. Though encased in morality and forced into the depths of the subconscious, our basic urges have an uncanny way of eventually resurfacing, claiming the weak and the strong, the rich and the poor, the reputable and the disreputable, and the least suspecting.

Repression or denial of one of the four basic urges often leads to an imbalance in one or more of the other three, initiating abnormal behavior or *displacement activities*. Displacement activities are compulsive behaviors used to ease the anxiety associated with repression of an urge. This progression can be outlined as follows:

Repression of Basic Urges
↓
Sublimation of Urges
↓
Displacement Activities
(often addictive/obsessive/compulsive behaviors)

Any activity that becomes excessive and hinders a person's ability to work or relate to others is a compulsion or addiction. Thoughts that become a nuisance or hindrance are obsessions.

Animals in captivity (repression of natural behaviors) often overeat, become oversexed, harm themselves and other animals, and pace about compulsively. In humans, displacement activities can range from minor behaviors, such as tapping a foot or biting fingernails, to the more serious and harmful behaviors such as drug abuse and violence. Although the gravity of the acts may vary, the mechanics of their development is the same.

Compulsions and addictions fill the gap between the body and the mind—between our expectations and reality. Compulsive behavior with food or alcohol (feed) may be triggered by repression of a sexual urge (fuck). An aggressive/hyperactive child (fight) may be suffering from a nutritional problem (feed), such as too many food additives or excessive sugar. Anxiety or phobias (flight) may be caused by food, alcohol or drugs (feed), sexual problems (fuck), or repressed anger (fight). Children may become addicted to television and snacks due to anxiety (flight) stemming from an angry or abusive parent (fight). Your mate may be obsessed with sports (fight) due to feeling inadequate/insecure (flight) in the bedroom (fuck). His sexual addiction (fuck) may be stemming from anxiety (flight) caused by problems at work (fight). Perhaps an unpleasant situation with your boss (fight/flight) is partly responsible for your weight problem (feed). Your teen-age daughter may disregard your admonition to avoid pregnancy (fuck) due to her repressed anger (fight) toward you. The point is: We all make choices based largely upon our urges, and these urges are influenced by those around us.

Compulsive or addictive behavior is often contagious. Someone married to an alcoholic may become compulsive with work to compensate for the anxiety felt while being around the alcoholic. A woman's compulsion with fantasy (romance novels, etc.) may serve as an escape from her husband's abusive or passive-aggressive behavior. An integrated system soon develops that begins feeding on itself.

This is the very repression/compulsion cycle that has made us a compulsive, obsessive, addictive society. Unfortunately, each generation inherits higher levels of anxiety and compulsion from the previous generation and our social problems compound.

Urge Disorders

Fight	(dopamine)	**Flight**
Abusive Behavior		Anxiety/Insecurity
Antisocial Behavior		Phobias/Fears
Possessiveness		Guilt/Shame
Envy (things)		Superstition
Overprotectiveness		Avoidance/Denial
Superiority Complex		Depression
Work/Sports-aholism		Obsessions/Compulsions
Criticism		Hypochondria
Homicide		Thrill-seeking
		Suicide

Rape/Sexual Abuse

Feed	(endorphins)	**Fuck**
Eating Disorders		Sexual Problems/Deviations
Smoking		Narcissism
Alcoholism		Dysmorphophobia
Drug Addiction		Envy (person)
Constipation/Diarrhea		Infertility/Impotence

29

Sympathetic (fight, flight) overloads often cause parasympathetic (feed, fuck) imbalances. Since the parasympathetic nerves largely control the digestive tract (feed), constipation can stem from repressed anger (fight), or diarrhea from anxiety (flight). Dietary or sexual problems (parasympathetics) can tense muscles (sympathetics), causing back pain or headaches: the psychosomatic connection.

This cross-over pattern also occurs with behavior. Abnormal acts such as rape and molestation are combinations of urges. Rape is largely an act of aggression (fight): taking control. The repressed urge to conquer or overpower displaces into the sexual realm and triggers rape or sexual abuse. A high percentage of child molesters were sexually abused as children. Later, their pent-up or repressed anger and insecurity/fear are unleashed upon other innocent children.

Many rapists and child molesters have readily-available outlets for sex, such as a wife or girlfriend, but choose instead to release their pent up urges upon an unsuspecting or resistant victim. The high or thrill comes from overcoming the barriers, not just the act itself. In fact, anxiety (flight) is the fuel for most addictions and compulsions. Shoplifting, robbery, extortion, drive-by shootings, dare-devil antics, etc., all feed off of the thrill associated with getting away with something, challenging the taboo, flirting with death.

There is another interesting phenomenon to consider. Over time the body recognizes and recalls the common sights, sounds, smells, situations, surroundings, time of day, etc., associated with an addictive or compulsive behavior. Consequently, the body's chemistry is triggered or queued into action before the behavior actually occurs (anticipation). Even though a behavior may be purposefully avoided, the body often reacts as if it is taking place.

This reaction is due, in part, to the body's self-preservation instinct or defense system. We are programmed to remember both harmful and pleasurable experiences so that similar subsequent events can be met with a greater degree of preparedness. Although this "recall" system helps to assure our survival, it reinforces addictive behaviors and raises anxiety levels.

Sadly, some people become compulsively contrary so they can experience the emotional stimulation associated with conflict. They sabotage the plans of others, consistently offer opposing opinions, throw temper tantrums, or resort to passive-aggressive tactics in their attempts to upset the apple cart. While these acts may be used initially to gain attention or control, they later become addictive due to the associated anxiety and emotional stimulation provided by the alternating dissension and reconciliation—the highs and the lows.

Our brains come equipped with pain-killing and pleasure systems—most notably, the dopamine and endorphin systems. Dopamine is more closely associated with our sympathetic urges and resembles the effects cocaine and amphetamines have on our bodies: stimulation/alertness. The endorphins are associated with our parasympathetic side and resemble the effects of alcohol, tranquilizers and painkillers (sedation/analgesia). This helps to explain why sex, for example, can temporarily ease pain and suffering— both mental and physical. A recent study has shown sex to be effective in relieving headaches in women.

These natural pleasure systems cause us to become addicted to various displacement activities. When we become anxious, we often engage in a repetitive behavior to ease our tension. Research has shown that these repetitive actions— or thoughts—trigger the release of endorphins into our system, which, as mentioned, sedate and relax us.

A nervous individual may tap his foot or bite his fingernails. Someone else may light up a cigarette. With smoking, the pleasure comes from both the activity (behavior) and the nicotine. Ironically, a recent study has shown that giving up smoking results in measurably lower stress levels, yet smokers continue to smoke, claiming they feel tense without a cigarette.

Eating is a means of escape for some people. A survey conducted at the Renfrew Center in Philadelphia found that 60 percent of eating disorder patients had been victims of violence, molestation, incest, or rape. Considering that an estimated one-third of American women have experienced some form of sexual abuse (fight + fuck), the prevalence of eating disorders among women is not surprising. The repressed anger (fight) and anxiety (flight) are simply displacing into the feed/endorphin pleasure system.

The male equivalent of anorexia or bulimia is an exaggerated drive to attain physical fitness or athletic achievement (dopamine system), including lower golf scores. Women, too, become obsessed with fitness, mostly to improve their appearance. Some are double addicted and vacillate between eating (endorphins) and purging/exercising (dopamine). Giving up one addiction may worsen the other.

Compulsions and obsessions (displacement activities) also provide a means of escape from the stress and pain associated with a bad relationship. Instead of addressing the problem and seeking a solution, we often find it easier to channel our anxiety into destructive thoughts and behaviors. But once we understand this process and can identify the true source of our anxiety, solutions come easier and we can begin to interact with our partner instead of avoid him. We also learn not to attack or condemn his compulsions, addictions, or inappropriate behaviors, since criticism only reinforces them.

Compulsive or addictive behaviors are often progressive, and have to be escalated and expanded over time to achieve the same level of gratification. This is especially true of sex, fantasy and chemical addictions. A level of accomodation takes place in the nervous system that subsequently requires higher levels of stimuli to achieve the same level of satisfaction. Consequently, a vicious cycle develops that becomes difficult to break.

When preoccupations get out of hand and become physical in nature, as is true for alcoholism and drug abuse, medical care may also be necessary to affect a cure. But the success of the treatment depends largely upon *behavioral modification.*

The escalation in violence (fight) worldwide is largely the result of anxiety stemming from repressed urges. Although murder and homicide may be motivated by the fear of being harmed or captured (self-defensive behaviors), some people, such as serial killers, kill purely for the thrill (adrenaline/dopamine) associated with the premeditation and the climax of the act itself. These "sick" individuals are addicted to their own anxiety and, unfortunately, sacrifice innocent people to get their "fix."

The fear of losing companionship (feed) or a sexual partner (fuck) motivates some people to commit murder. We quickly become dependent upon those who help to satisfy our basic urges, and letting go of them can be quite unsettling.

Studies have revealed that acts of violence are more likely to occur when the blood sugar level is low or while the individual is under the influence of alcohol or drugs (feed). Violent individuals often exhibit higher levels of testosterone, which is affected to some degree by diet. All of this underscores the fact that the *feed* urge strongly influences our behavior.

Problems in the economy and the associated cutbacks also contribute to increased violence, since unemployed men lose a significant means of expressing their *fight* urge. Mass killers often are recently unemployed, disgruntled individuals.

In domestic violence, abusive men often say that their

mates deserved it, or that *she needed to be put in her place.* These men have the perception that their mates have gotten the upper hand in the relationship and are becoming too independent. Such men are often insecure (flight) and exhibit exaggerated levels of possessiveness (fight) and jealousy (fuck). Unfortunately, the only solution they can see is to be-become abusive and retake control.

As a woman becomes more independent, her mate's value as a provider and protector diminishes. If he's an insecure and anxious person, his responsive behavior may be retaliatory and violent. A woman finding herself in this situation should tread softly—right out the door and never look back! No one deserves physical abuse, and violent men are not likely to change.

During their courtship Bonnie was attracted to Steve's independence and charm. But after they were married his displays of anger began to concern her. As a teen-ager, Steve had been a bit of a troublemaker, pulling pranks on others and teasing a lot. Yet he had been pretty good to Bonnie while they were dating in high school, and she was impressed by his displays of superiority over the other boys in their class. Steve was a good athlete and had little trouble attracting girls, so Bonnie felt privileged and special when he chose her to be his girlfriend, and later his wife.

But, now, Steve was not so appealing to Bonnie. He had become a workaholic, and was growing increasingly irritable and volatile. During an argument one evening he slapped her across the face. Bonnie couldn't believe it. Her Prince Charming had become an ogre. When her repeated attempts to convince Steve to seek counseling failed, and the verbal and physical abuse escalated, she mustered up her courage and left him. Although this was a difficult decision, her life was better for it.

♥ ♥ ♥

Remaining in an abusive relationship is life-threatening. As of this writing, nearly four thousand women die of domestic violence annually, and FBI reports show that 30 percent of women murdered in the United States are killed by husbands or boyfriends. More women seek medical care for injuries resulting from domestic violence than for rape, mugging, and auto accidents combined.

The highest rates of domestic violence are among professional men who value social status and believe that their wives are holding them back. In fact, couples with lower educational levels are *less* prone to violence. The second-highest group is working-class men who believe in male superiority but are married to a woman with a better job. These men resent the fact that their wives are higher on the financial ladder (fight/competition). One study revealed that *both* partners are less likely to be satisfied with the relationship if the wife has more status and authority. This helps to explain why housewives are less likely to be beaten than working women.

Power struggles between men and women cause more domestic violence than poverty, unemployment, alcoholism, and childhood abuse combined. Though alcoholics are four times more likely to beat their wives, violence generally continues at the same level after completion of an alcohol treatment program.

Women's increased independence has led to a commensurate rise in violence toward women. Female independence threatens men's identity and raises their anxiety level, which, in turn, predisposes them to violent behaviors and predatory acts. A recent study by Linda Carli of the College of the Holy Cross found that women, from homemakers to executives, are more likely to get what they want from men by subtly assuming a second-class status. Attempting to persuade through the traditional male avenues of intimidation or superiority is not as productive. Although this may seem unfair, it is better for a woman to operate accordingly than to go through life naively expecting men always to treat her as an equal. Remember: *Sometimes we win by losing.* Men's basic identity is determined by genetics, and changes are not likely to occur for perhaps several generations—*if ever.*

Diane, age 33, decided to go back to work as a nurse once her children started grade school. Stan, her husband, disliked that decision, since it meant his responsibilities around the house would increase and he would lose some of the conveniences he had grown accustomed to. He had been raised in a family where the women stayed home and kept house. Dinner was always on time, mom made the beds, and the men did few household chores. Although this was not a factor when he first married Diane, Stan's expectations of a wife following in his mother's footsteps surfaced once the children came along. Diane was eager to be at home with the kids and didn't mind giving up her job, since Stan's income as an accountant was sufficient to maintain their standard of living.

Stan and Diane got along well in the traditional family style until the children entered school and Diane experienced the Empty Nest Syndrome. With the children at home all day, Diane had kept busy and did not have much time to think about her own needs. But now she missed feeling needed and receiving recognition for her efforts. As a nurse at the hospital she had always felt a part of a team. She got respect, and others depended upon her. She also enjoyed the excitement associated with life-and-death situations.

To minimize any strain from the transition, Diane had taken great care in formulating her plan to return to work, including checking out local day-care centers for the children. Having lost her seniority she would have to work some odd shifts, and she was counting on Stan to pick up the kids when she couldn't. Everything was set, except Stan.

Once Stan heard the plan his behavior began to deteriorate. He countered with a list of objections that ranged from the children's needs to his ability to provide well for his family. Although his concerns were valid, Stan actually resented the fact that Diane would be spending a lot of time around successful doctors—some of them single men. Stan didn't admit this to Diane, but he figured that if he could keep her at home, the chances of her having an affair would be slim.

Stan's fear of abandonment, which is a human's greatest fear, clashed with Diane's need for acceptance, appreciation, and admiration—a human's greatest desire. As they continued to defend their positions on the matter, a wall of resentment rose between them that quickly obscured their view of each other's needs. Ironically, despite Stan's fear of losing Diane, his attempts to keep her actually drove her away and they eventually divorced. Diane went back to work—this time from necessity—and Stan took up with a younger woman who, oddly enough, had a career and exhibited very little in the way of domestic skills.

The moral of this story is that what seems to be the main issue may not be the true issue after all. What we often hold out to be important to us may change with the circumstances. Although Stan suffered from the fear of losing his wife—and eventually from the pain of a divorce—he managed to emerge from it all in pursuit of another woman with the very qualities he had previously opposed.

A man's expectations of a woman tend to be lower when he is actively pursuing her. Then, once she has committed to him and he is in control, his expectations of her begin to rise. In essence, she has allowed herself to become his possession, and he has gladly assumed ownership of her. If she decides to escape—become more independent—he becomes defensive and his expectations of her increase. Little issues become big issues as he vies to regain control.

Ideally, men would always be understanding and sympathetic toward a woman's needs and wishes. Yet, through expectations formed from growing up in a traditional family, through the media's depiction of what is normal, or perhaps even through biology—which we know can dictate roles and behaviors—some men innately feel that they should be in charge, and that a woman best serves humanity by being a mother and a sex machine. Most women do not agree with this ideology and consider it idiocy.

Although men have traditionally been labeled as the abusers, several recent studies have revealed that women assault their mates nearly as often as men do. According to sociologist Murray Straus, codirector of the Family Research Laboratory at the University of New Hampshire, a man *and* a woman are physically abused every 18 seconds.

Regardless of the origin of this conflict between men and women, it runs deep. Though men's awareness of women's rights has risen in the last few decades, crimes and violence against women by men have increased. Sensitive men may publicly sympathize with women's issues, but many secretly harbor resentment toward the female's increasing autonomy. The overriding factor preventing them from expressing their resentment in a violent or abusive manner is their need for women to accept them. Without this buffering agent, more men would come down hard on women.

Since males are biologically programmed to be the providers and protectors, and the female's expanding autonomy ultimately renders this identity invalid, it follows that men would greet the women's movement with some level of resistance and retaliation.

Instead of living a life of frustration and disappointment waiting for men to change, a woman can secure a comfortable lifestyle for herself by facing reality and operating within the laws of human nature. This does not mean becoming a doormat, but it does require adopting a new attitude toward men and reacting differently to them: *working smart.*

The ideal relationship is one in which the female is truly in charge, but the male believes *he* is! As my grandmother used to say: "Give a man enough rope to hang himself, then cut him down. He'll be forever grateful."

With a better understanding of what triggers men into negative behavior a woman can begin to minimize conflict with her mate, as well as structure an environment that is conducive to eliciting positive behavior from him. Although research shows that a person's basic personality can rarely be permanently changed, positive behaviors *can* be enhanced to such a degree that negative ones are overshadowed.

Possessiveness causes problems in many relationships, as we discovered in the case of Stan and Diane. Although possessiveness seems to be a negative trait, it does have merit and comes as a standard feature in all relationships. As shown in the basic urge chart of various behaviors, *fight, flight, feed,* and *fuck* all contribute to bonding—and bonding denotes an element of dependence. As we become dependent upon someone or something, we become protective and possessive. Since possessiveness often incites anger and aggressive countermeasures when we appear to be losing someone or something we have bonded to, I have included possessiveness in the list of *fight* behaviors.

Animals also exhibit possessiveness, such as a dog protecting a formerly abandoned bone when another dog tries to take it. Children also reclaim a previously discarded toy when discovered in the hands of another. Possessiveness is a part of nature's survival plan, reinforcing the bonding process and ensuring protection of possessions, such as food, shelter, or the money to buy those things. Possessiveness became biologically ingrained because of early humankind's competitive environment and the need to protect limited food supplies and possessions from the elements and outsiders.

Experts caution us against becoming too attached to or possessive of our partners, yet our level of bonding is directly proportional to our dependence. Attempting to avoid becoming too attached to them is to go against our nature.

The possession-obsession trait does get out of hand at times, especially following the discovery of infidelity—or in the case of separation or divorce—as a person begins to sense the impending loss (possessiveness) and accompanying insecurity (anxiety). The resulting tension evokes volatile behavior that may erupt in violence. Some people kill to protect what they have or are in fear of losing. Others destroy lives and property out of spite, rationalizing that, "If I can't have it, no one else can!" Nothing is held back, and children are often used as a weapon or threat in order to gain control over a partner.

Our behavior is under the control of four interdependent factors:

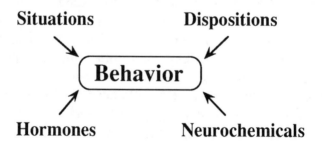

Situations   **Dispositions**

Behavior

Hormones   **Neurochemicals**

Hormones and neurochemicals (nerve transmitter substances) cannot be controlled at whim by the average person, except with medication. Also, personality—one's general disposition—is largely determined by genetics and cannot be permanently altered. Therefore, the only remaining factor readily available to influence another person's behavior is *situations*.

Situations can be created or altered by manipulating reality—meaning the environment or the circumstances. By altering a person's perception, we ultimately influence his behavior. This can be a very valuable tool when reality cannot be changed. *To the magician there is no magic, just altered perceptions of reality.*

Perception can be changed through education, provided the individual is willing to accept new information, or by playing on basic urges. When we encounter someone who is resistant to our wishes, and we cannot influence him simply through education or communication, we often resort to motivating him through his basic urges (fight, flight, feed, and fuck). We all do this inadvertently and unconsciously on many occasions in our daily lives, but the key is to understand fully how these principles work and when to use them.

Some people are adept at this game and can easily persuade others to believe or behave a certain way. For example, advertisers and movie producers realize that to maximize impact and to assure adequate motivation of the consumer, all four urges must be activated. The more senses (sight, sound, smell, taste, touch) stimulated, the better, since they modulate our urges. Successful productions include depictions of *fight* (violence, competition, heroism), *flight* (danger, suspense), *feed* (eating, drinking, smoking, alcohol, and drugs), and last, but not least, *fuck* (sex).

Other vendors benefit from this exposure as well. When we watch a movie, for example, we repress our urges due to confinement in a movie theater or living room in the company of others who might be disturbed by our normal reactions. This results in anxiety, which displaces into other activities that *are* more socially acceptable, such as stuffing ourselves with candy and popcorn and drinking too much soda or beer.

Unfortunately, some people use the power of the basic urges to manipulate and deceive others in a selfish attempt to control or profit. Some attack through the *fight* mode and demand what they want. Others use intimidation or threats (flight), and some try to bribe with food (feed) or sex (fuck). I firmly believe that these behaviors are at the root of our social ills.

As long as we continue to be a restrictive, proscriptive society void of healthy alternatives through which urges can be expressed, as well as a society whose expectations far exceed what reality can deliver, anxiety levels will remain high. In turn, food, alcohol, tobacco, pornography, and drug dealers will continue to flourish. Prisons, casinos, psychiatrists' offices, and divorce courts will remain full. And multitudes of people will keep spending their last few dollars on a ticket to the movies, the ball-game, or the lottery. (Obsessive-compulsive disorders are estimated to be fifty times more prevalent than once believed.)

If, on the other hand, we understand and acknowledge the power of our basic urges, and use them in a positive fashion, we can extract ourselves from our current predicament. It will take a while for global changes to occur, but our own lives can be improved practically overnight.

Love Is A Many Splendored Thing

5

$\mathcal{A}$s previously mentioned, jealousy consists largely of a sexual component (fuck) for men, and a fear of being replaced or a loss of companionship (feed) for women. These emotions are consistent with the basic nature of males and females. Considering that our urges largely comprise our nature and are intimately connected to our natural pleasure systems, we can now explain why men and women become addicted to sex and relationships—or almost anything.

And yet addictions are a part of the bonding process. We become attached to another person out of his or her ability to satisfy our basic needs and stimulate our pleasure systems. Many things play a part in the bonding process, even body odors. But our primary attraction to another is largely due to his or her ability to satisfy, or help us express, our four basic urges.

In essence, we can define love as: *A merging of the basic urges of two individuals*.

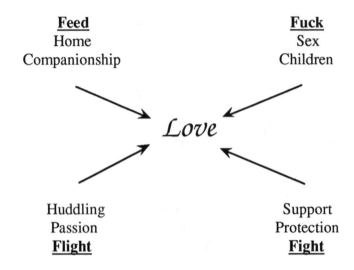

Feed
Home
Companionship

Fuck
Sex
Children

Love

Huddling
Passion
Flight

Support
Protection
Fight

Love is a term applied to many kinds of relationships. In a male-female relationship it encompasses mutual respect, protection, support, and a sharing of money and possessions (fight). It involves huddling—drawing together out of fear and insecurity—and passion (flight). It includes companionship and establishing a home (feed). It entails sexual pleasure and having children (fuck).

Surveys of couples who have divorced reveal that, besides infidelity, women most often cite unreasonable behavior and a breakdown in communication as the reasons the union failed. Men tend to blame sexual staleness and the need for "space." Both sexes also report that criticism (fight) was a major problem, but criticism is only a secondary reaction and a symptom of some underlying problem. This leaves us with a lack of intimacy and satisfying sex as the primary concerns of men and women.

To most women, intimacy is synonymous with communication and companionship. For them—contrary to their male counterparts—sex is not the primary source of intimacy. Women perceive intimacy as more of a sharing of activities than of bodies—discourse rather than intercourse. According to an Ann Landers survey: Given the choice between simply cuddling or having sex with their mates for the rest of their lives, most women favor cuddling.

Men's image of intimacy is sexual. To them, cuddling is okay, but only as an overture to the sex act, which is consistent with their primary urge: *fuck*. This perspective difference between men and women gives conflicting meanings to the word *love*. From a man's perspective it means being a good provider (fight) and sex partner (fuck)—things that don't require much time devoted directly to building the relationship. To women, love means close companionship and good communication (feed), which are things that involve a considerable time commitment and extensive proximity. That's why men often feel capable of *loving* several women at one time, while most women have difficulty imagining such a thing.

The perceptions each sex has of love and the responsibilities associated with maintaining it are different. This explains why each sex often takes the love contributions of the other for granted. The title of a currently popular book, *Why Men Don't Get Enough Sex and Women Don't Get Enough Love,* says it all.

Deep love encompasses the higher human urges of inquisitiveness, playfulness, laughter, weeping, creativity, spirituality, etc. These factors give deep love its full and rich spectrum of emotions and feelings.

But one cannot experience *deep* love if *basic* love is not complete and balanced. Too many individuals become disenchanted from not experiencing higher love when, in reality, they have not built the foundation necessary for attaining such heights. Once a relationship is structured so that each person's basic urges are adequately satisfied, it becomes easier to cross over into the greener pastures of *deep* love.

Humans have a hierarchy of needs. Psychologist Abraham Maslow identified these needs as *physiological, safety, esteem,* and *self-actualization.*

Maslow's Model of Needs

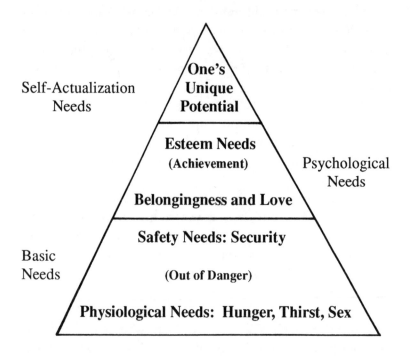

According to Maslow, humans must first have their physiological needs met before higher needs can be realized. Before the higher human urges of creativity, spirituality, self-actualization, deep love, etc., can be attained and maintained, *basic* urges and needs must be satisfied. Fundamental needs include physiological and safety considerations.

Physiological requirements include such things as air, food, water, and sex. Safety needs include clothing and shelter. Above this level are psychological needs, such as belongingness and love, which encompass some of the fundamental needs. Next are esteem needs or individual achievement, which, again, depend upon the preceding factors. And, finally, self-actualization needs that motivate us to attain our unique potential.

If we use Maslow's model of needs to define relationships we can construct the following:

Maslow's Model of Needs
(Relationship Levels)

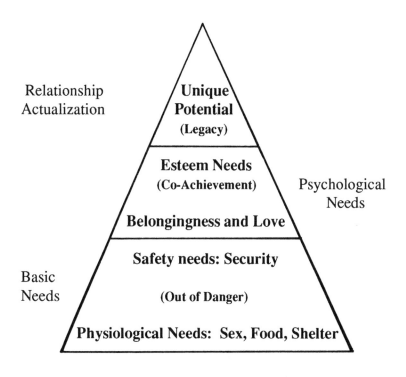

Relationship
Actualization

**Unique
Potential**
(Legacy)

Esteem Needs
(Co-Achievement)

Psychological
Needs

Belongingness and Love

Safety needs: Security

Basic
Needs

(Out of Danger)

Physiological Needs: Sex, Food, Shelter

In forming a relationship the needs of two individuals must merge. Relationships provide access to basic needs, such as companionship, sex, and having children. Joining with another is symbiotic. We seek out other people to satisfy our needs, and simultaneously we attempt to satisfy theirs. If Maslow is correct, we cannot attain our unique potential without the contributions of other people along the way. We ally with others to improve our access to the things we need or find pleasurable. When we proclaim our commitment to a relationship we are, in fact, acknowledging our dependence upon it.

To attain the higher levels of fulfillment or pleasure in life, and perhaps to leave a legacy as a successful couple, our basic needs must first be met. And those needs are largely interdependent. Once a couple has devised a plan that allows for mutual satisfaction of their basic urges, higher levels of achievement, harmony and contentment can be realized. If, on the other hand, they attempt to ascend to the higher levels without first constructing a good foundation, any success is likely to be compromised by the conflict arising from the unstable base. If too much instability is present the relationship may collapse.

This is also true of some of the popular self-improvement or success programs that stress projecting oneself into the higher human states of creativity, positive mental attitude, playfulness, and spirituality. Proponents of these programs, as well as some religions, stress ignoring primitive urges and, instead, focusing on higher ideals. Although forcing oneself to have a positive mental attitude can improve various aspects of one's life, if steps aren't concurrently taken to assure satisfaction of the basic urges, any achievements may eventually fall through a weak spot in the foundation and shatter. Unfortunately, a lot of well-intentioned individuals ride a wave of sublimity for a time only to sink back into an ocean of despair as a result of neglecting their basic needs, and the basic needs of those around them.

The current popularity of labeling someone as co-dependent is fallacious, since life itself is a codependent proposition. Of course, everyone should be encouraged to take steps to assure a healthy level of self-sufficiency and to avoid being taken advantage of. But to foster a notion that you can be totally independent and yet committed to a relationship is contradictory. When we consider that the divorce rate and many of our other social ills have paralleled the independence movement, promoting high levels of autonomy may be detrimental to society. Especially when the price of our pleasure is often someone else's pain. The problem is not that we become too dependent, it's that we become too dependent upon undependable people.

Living With The Enemy

6

*A*nger and fear may not be ideal emotions, but they are necessary to our existence. The *fight* urge serves to protect us in threatening situations by activating and coordinating the body systems involved in self-defense. But sometimes this urge gets out of hand and becomes destructive to both lives and relationships. There is overwhelming evidence that higher levels of anger result in higher death rates, illness, social isolation, and less success at work and love.

According to Joseph Wolpe, M.D., noted psychiatrist and author of *Life Without Fear,* the root cause of anger is **anxiety**. This means that our *fight* urge is largely under the control of our *flight* urge. Before we can reduce or eliminate anger we must first reduce or eliminate the underlying anxiety. Contrary to popular opinion, recent studies have found that expressing anger is not cathartic and often leads to more anger. Until the source of the anger is eliminated, screaming, pounding your pillow, the wall, or another person is not likely to make things better. This is substantiated by the behavior of criminals who continue in their established pattern of violent acts as long as the cause of their aggression persists.

Despite the negative aspects of anger, a certain amount of arguing (fight) in a relationship appears necessary to establish or maintain rank, territory, and the right to exist and transact. Without this ability to set boundaries, one person would likely take over complete control of the other, which we see too often. By confronting and reacting to our partner's offensive actions with positive defensive countermeasures, we communicate and delineate our needs and desires. Also, we learn what our partner's needs and desires are, and how they rank in priority with ours.

Although arguing creates much tension for a couple it provides stimulation and shows that there is still some concern for the relationship—a desire to make it better. The real danger occurs when apathy sets in, when a couple no longer cares enough to voice needs and concerns. Don't feel badly about periodic arguing. It's okay. Just make sure it's over new issues, not old, worn out ones. The key to resolving worn-out debates is to identify the underlying anxiety and eliminate it.

When arguing is inevitable, or necessary to get across one's opinion, here are some simple rules to follow that won't turn a constructive discussion into a full-fledged battle:

Avoid Using Judgmental Phrases Such As:

"You should have..."
"You didn't..."
"You always..."
"You never..."
"How could you..."
"Why didn't you..."
"I knew you would..."

Such phrases are highly critical and accusatory, and only serve to elicit defensive behavior or a negative response.

Criticism
Reinforces negative behavior
#1 cause of relapses into compulsive behaviors
#1 cause of drop-out from treatment programs

In attempting to rectify a slight we like to place the blame as quickly and poignantly as possible. Unfortunately, this just shuts down the recipient and prevents him from objectively evaluating his alleged misconduct or misdeed. If, on the other hand, we simply say we are upset and give the reason, much of the defensiveness is avoided, and the other person will be more apt to move into an objective frame of mind and reflect upon his injurious actions.

To be more effective in getting your mate to respond to your needs and requests, use phrases such as:

> **"I'm upset because..."**
> **"You hurt me by..."**
> **"I feel that..."**
> **"I'm concerned about..."**
> **"I would appreciate..."**
> **"I would respect you more if..."**

This approach to the problem does not activate the fight/ flight mechanism to quite the extent that direct accusations do, and the other person is more likely to feel remorseful and to be more considerate of his actions in the future. Sadly, many women stifle their mate's power and creativity through criticism, instead of nurturing those proclivities to their mutual benefit.

Breaking old habits is hard to do, and we often react improperly. But over time with practice, old, ineffective habits can be broken and new, effective strategies can be implemented. We may be able to blame others for our start in life, but we can only blame ourselves for the finish. In other words, someone may have dealt us the cards, but *we* choose how to play our hand.

We have heard that everything should be equal in a relationship, but this is neither realistic nor practical. Ideally, power and control vacillate between the partners in equal measure, with each perhaps being more responsible and accountable in certain areas based on experience and expertise. Unfortunately, this is often easier said than done—especially when the attempt to control is based on emotion instead of reason.

Arguments in a relationship commonly center on the time-honored subjects of money, children, sex, and household chores. Yet these are just battlegrounds for underlying issues, such as *power* and *control*. As resentment increases in a relationship, due to unmet needs or expectations, anxiety levels rise (flight) and aggressiveness increases (fight). This perceived loss of control, which is the cause of the anxiety, results in attempts to regain control.

As anxiety increases, so do levels of expectation. Things that were previously benign suddenly become malignant. Hair in the sink, towels on the floor, and shoes not put away all become serious issues and fodder for debate. One person may lash out with anger and criticism in an attempt to express built-up resentment and to exert some control. The other person may react to the situation with passive aggression (fight + flight) and withdraw to pout, which is another form of control.

Regardless of the response to the situation, the important thing to recognize is that the breakdown of a relationship begins with an increase in anxiety (flight) but ends with expressions of anger (fight). Therefore, locating the source of the increase in anxiety reveals the cause of the relationship's turmoil and eventual demise. Focusing our attention on the anger or aggression delays getting to the underlying issue.

Money problems (fight) are blamed for the failure of many relationships. Yet there are examples of couples drawn together during financial difficulties by the common goals formulated to rise above their predicament. In some cases, once the financial crisis passed and funds were abundant, the relationship may have failed. Money, of itself, does not drive a couple apart. It simply widens the cracks already present in the relationship. Since money is a symbol of power and control, it easily becomes a weapon on the battlefields of life and love.

Considering that anxiety arises from a threat or loss of control, and much of men's anxiety stems from work and sex, a woman is not likely to improve her relationship with her mate if she competes with him as a breadwinner or jilts him sexually. Studies show that couples are more likely to divorce or separate when the female earns more than the male.

Joan and Michael were having difficulties. Married for six years with no children, they were on their way up the ladder of success and enjoyed an active lifestyle. Joan, a corporate attorney for a large manufacturer, was earning considerably more money than Michael, an accountant in private practice. Although their marriage had started out with a lot of zip and zing, it now was fizzling. Michael was often moody and withdrawn, which caused Joan to be more critical and demanding of him.

Although he was reluctant to admit it, Michael resented

the fact that Joan made more money than he did. He disliked being dependent upon her. He had hoped that his accounting business would grow and eventually provide him with a higher income than Joan's. Playing the role of the liberated man, Michael had tried his best to repress his envy and resentment. But with his business at a standstill and Joan continuing to move up the corporate ladder, he was viewing her more as a foe than an ally.

Joan knew that Michael was unhappy about the lack of growth in his company, but didn't realize how much she was contributing to his frustration by failing to validate his efforts to provide for her. After attending one of my seminars she began to understand the dynamics of Michael's resentment and moodiness, and she formulated a plan to heal their relationship.

First, Joan got Michael to answer the *Ten-Questionnaire* I developed for couples interested in improving their relationships (see page 176). This exercise helped him define his goals and expectations for his life and marriage. Next, Joan began showing concern for Michael's business and offered to help him make it better. She was careful not to convey the impression that he had failed and she was going to rescue him.

Joan sought out marketing strategies for businesses such as Michael's and then presented them to him in a casual way when he seemed open and receptive. When he expressed interest in a particular strategy, Joan offered to help him set it up, including diverting some of her income to the project. Expressing her excitement over the chance of seeing Michael's business grow helped to rebuild his confidence and self-image. With a new approach and a change of attitude his business began to take off, and his relationship with Joan improved.

Joan was proud of her part in the success story, but she only let Michael know how proud she was of *him*. Boasting about *her* efforts would only create tension and project them back into their previous predicament. Seeing Michael become a different person was reward enough for her.

A woman who earns more than her mate will usually find that she has to put forth extra effort to validate his contributions. Men are not programmed to appreciate being financially supported: it undermines their sense of self-worth.

Making a man feel appreciated and admired is a requisite in the mating game. Simply saying *thank you*, or *I'm proud of you*, makes a tremendous difference, as does a gift or flowers accompanied by a thank-you note.

When resentment exists, or a mate fails to reciprocate, saying *thank you* may be difficult. Yet failing to do so may allow the relationship to dissolve. Men are very proud of their ability to provide, and if their mates don't validate that effort, perhaps another woman will.

Anxiety for a woman stems largely from her efforts to maintain her appearance and personal relationships. Thus the *feed* and *fuck* urges are the primary sources of *her* unhappiness. But before we take a closer look at these urges, let's finish our discussion of *fight* and *flight*.

Anxiety is the enemy, causing us to fall prey to unhealthy alternatives to reality. Research on anxiety (stress) has shown it to be the root of most human maladies—both physical and social. Anxiety is cumulative, and, if chronic, it can lead to major illness by the early forties.

Problems in the *fight, feed*, or *fuck* urges invariably translate into increased anxiety (flight). *Flight* is the garbage dump for problems arising from the other three urges. We get it from all directions, as depicted by the following chart—which is by no means complete:

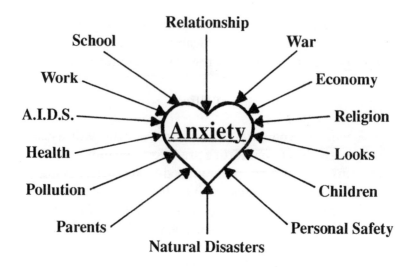

Here is a simple formula to calculate your level of anxiety:

$$\text{Anxiety} = \text{Expectations} - \text{Reality}$$
$$\text{(Want)} \qquad \text{(Have)}$$

Since the underlying cause of anger is anxiety, we also can use this formula for our level of anger—or even disappointment. If our expectations consistently exceed what reality can deliver, we become anxious, angry, and disappointed.

Men and women have gender-specific areas of performance anxiety that are consistent with their identities and expectations:

Men: Work & Sex
Women: Appearance & Relationships

As our level of anxiety increases, so does self-centeredness and self-consciousness, which is due to our self-preservation instinct. When we encounter situations or circumstances that make us anxious—a real or perceived threat, or a real or perceived loss of control—the body's natural reaction is to create a heightened sense of self-awareness via the sympathetic nervous system (fight/flight). This increased self-consciousness or self-centeredness serves to put us on guard in truly threatening situations, but it can get out of hand, giving rise to selfish, possessive, or demanding behavior. As patience and tolerance diminish, common courtesy fades. When this occurs on a wide scale in a society, terms like *The Me Generation* crop up.

Anxiety is three-dimensional. It stems from real or perceived threats from the past, the present, or the future. We also inherit a slightly higher baseline level of anxiety from our ancestors. In other words, we come into this world with a slate that already has a few scribbles on it—in indelible ink. Then, as we record painful and stressful life events, our slate becomes cluttered and we have trouble reading our script. Just as with a school play when we cannot remember our lines, we panic and try to ad lib, often making no sense at all, confusing everyone and upsetting the entire production. To prevent this from happening in our life we must erase some of the confusion and uncertainty on our slate so that the important messages will be legible. This is accomplished by acquiring *knowledge* and *experience*—two important virtues that improve our lives and relationships.

The impact anxiety has upon us is largely dependent upon our *perception* and *interpretation* of the stressful events or emotions we have encountered, are encountering, or anticipate to encounter in the future—in essence, *our attitude.* If we can come to terms with our fears and resentments, put situations and events into proper perspective and avoid overreacting, great personal and interpersonal healing occurs.

I remember an incident with my children that caused me to realize how much our perception and behavior is influenced by the actions and reactions of those around us.

While on an outing with my family my oldest daughter, Angela, age eight at the time, suffered a deep laceration to her right index finger. She was bleeding profusely and became hysterical. I was alarmed as well, but managed to mask my anxiety to calm her down. I held her hand under running water and assured her that the bleeding would eventually stop, and that she was not going to die. I calmly explained that we were letting the finger bleed for a little while to wash out all the germs, and that bleeding is the body's way of cleaning out the wound. Her sobbing tapered off and she began to smile through tear-filled eyes. After a few minutes the bleeding slowed and I bandaged her finger. The cut healed nicely, leaving only a small scar.

I didn't realize the full impact my behavior would have on my daughter until a couple of years later when my son, Joel, who is four years younger than Angela, cut *his* finger. Angie was nearest him at the time and went to his aid. I overheard her repeating—practically word for word—the speech I had given to *her* a few years earlier. I stood back and allowed her to handle the situation. Her brother responded to her as she had to me, and he was soon calm.

It was then that I realized how much our behavior affects those around us, and how important it is that we don't overreact. Had I become hysterical at the sight of my daughter's cut, I would have only reinforced her fears. She, in turn, may have made a contribution to her brother's anxiety a few years later by overreacting as well. Since my middle child, Amber, witnessed her sister's behavior during their brother's crisis, she too learned an important lesson.

Events in our lives and relationships activate our emotions and stimulate certain behaviors. These behaviors usually carry consequences. In his book, *The Deadly Diet*, Terence Sandbek, Ph.D., outlines this progression for eating disorders. His outline is appropriate for all behaviors:

Event
↓
Emotions
↓
Behavior
↓
Consequences

When this progression results in negative consequences and is physically and/or emotionally harmful, it can be altered by introducing another factor between the event and the emotion. That factor is our *attitude*, or how we choose to interpret the event. Our attitude is the filter through which events must pass in order to evoke certain emotions. By changing our attitude about a situation we can alter our reaction to it and, ultimately, the consequences associated with it.

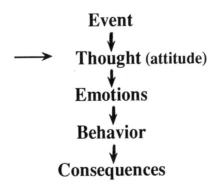

Event
↓
⟶ **Thought** (attitude)
↓
Emotions
↓
Behavior
↓
Consequences

When we consider an event to be negative, the body responds by activating the sympathetic nervous system. This, in turn, causes the body to produce adrenaline and cortisol, which, in excessive amounts, cause health problems. Events considered positive, on the other hand, produce health-promoting substances. Hence, our attitude toward life events largely determines our general health.

We become anxious in a given situation due to a lack of understanding or experience. Consequently, we may interpret things incorrectly and react inappropriately. The key to reducing anxiety is to *increase our knowledge and experience*. Remember when you were learning to ride a bicycle or drive a car? You were nervous and frustrated. But once you learned the rules and gained experience, your anxiety gradually diminished, and your confidence grew because you were in control.

This holds true for the male-female experience. When our partner behaves negatively toward us, perhaps for no obvious reason, we become frustrated and angry. The underlying anxiety stems from a real or perceived threat to our security, or a loss of control. Once we learn the causes of poor behavior and how we can influence it, our confidence and patience increase while anxiety and frustration decrease. Ironically, our partners did not change—and some never will—but we *changed our attitude* toward the situation and reacted accordingly. By changing one part of the equation, in this case *ourselves*, we automatically alter the results.

♥ ♥ ♥

Barbara and Neil had been married for five years. It was the second marriage for them both. Barbara's two children from her first marriage lived with them, while Neil's teenage daughter, Andrea, from his previous marriage lived with her mother. Things went pretty smoothly until Andrea would come to visit. Then, tension built.

Barbara had been seeing me for recurring headaches. When I asked her to list the sources of stress in her life, Andrea's name came up. Checking back in my records, I noticed that Barbara's bouts with headaches often coincided with Andrea's visits.

Barbara confided that she was resentful when Neil lavished Andrea with attention and money on her visits while ignoring the other two children. Neil and Andrea would go places and do things without inviting anyone along. Barbara had discussed this with Neil several times, but he usually got indignant and turned a cold shoulder to her complaint.

I had been through this situation myself and knew something about the emotions involved. Barbara didn't understand that Neil was feeling guilty about having left his daughter and her mother, and that he was simply buying some peace of mind through pleasing Andrea.

Seeing Neil playing sugar-daddy to someone besides her or her children made Barbara envious and jealous. She realized that Andrea's stay was only temporary, but Neil's behavior still bothered her. Neil, of course, was more concerned about pleasing Andrea, since doing so made him feel better about himself and his past mistakes. Had he consented to Barbara's wishes to repress his urge to pamper Andrea, he would eventually have taken out his frustration and resentment on Barbara and her children. He would have looked upon them as a barrier between himself and his own flesh and blood.

Meeting with Barbara and Neil cleared up much of the tension surrounding this problem. Neil told me that he and Andrea had never excluded Barbara and her children from their activities—Barbara had just refused to join them on their outings from the beginning, so Neil quit asking. Barbara admitted that she felt a little resentful toward Andrea since she represented Neil's past life with another woman—

a woman with whom he still had to have contact.

Barbara's insecurity and anxiety over the situation stemmed from the fear that Neil had not completely broken the bonds to his former wife. Down deep Barbara was afraid that someday Neil would go back to her, perhaps for Andrea's sake. Unfortunately, Barbara's attitude and behavior set up an environment for that very thing to occur. She was certainly justified in her complaint that Neil should do more to make her children feel accepted and appreciated, but she failed to recognize the part *she* was playing in bringing about this division of favor.

Neil choked back a few tears as he expressed disappointment over the inability to blend the two families. He admitted that the guilt surrounding his divorce had caused him to pay more attention to Andrea than Barbara's children, but since he was around Barbara's children on a daily basis he felt justified in giving Andrea some special attention.

I agreed with Neil on this point, but made him aware that he was now doing less with Barbara and her children than when they were dating. His initial involvement had set a higher level of expectation, which now was not being met, and Barbara was interpreting his decreased involvement as a waning of his love for her and her children.

Once reassured of Neil's devotion and convinced that he had no interest in rekindling a relationship with his former wife, Barbara's perception of the situation changed and her attitude toward Andrea and her visits improved considerably. This, in turn, strengthened her relationship with Neil, and, best of all, her headaches disappeared.

♥ ♥ ♥

Simple attitude changes can even heal wounds from the past. Lacking understanding or experience at a time in our life when we suffered an emotional trauma we may have repressed our anxiety. But as we mature and gain experience and understanding, our perception and interpretation capabilities improve, and we become more rational, realistic and accepting of our past. With these qualities expanded, we regain control of our lives, and, once in control, we are able to release the emotional emergency brake that has been holding us back.

Knowledge and experience also help to insulate us against the effects of current and future stress. Thus the benefits are three-dimensional: helping us resolve issues in our past; helping us deal with the present; and preparing us for the future. Understanding and experience foster patience and empathy, which, in turn, make it easier for us to forgive ourselves and others.

Sharing our knowledge and experience with someone helps us, too. When we see another person benefitting from our knowledge and experience, our self-esteem increases, and we focus less on our own troubles.

Apathy

Unfortunately, we have become so calloused to many of the prevalent abnormal situations and behaviors that our perception of normal is somewhat askew. We fail to respond when we should or we respond when we shouldn't. We even feel guilty and anxious when we don't find ourselves motivated to react or behave as others do. This stems largely from our fear of rejection.

The lowest and most dangerous state of mind is apathy. In this condition we have gone beyond the stages of anxiety and anger as the result of overstimulation or prolonged stress. This is also true of depression. We don't feel compelled to act or react when confronted with threats to our existence or to our relationship with another. We overeat, get drunk, take drugs, withdraw into a vegetative state, ignore family and friends—despite being aware of the consequences. We can even be selective in our apathy, reserving it for certain aspects of our lives or certain people, such as our mate, while expending great amounts of energy on other matters.

Our society is moving toward a state of apathy, or what I call "The Great Depression." All indicators seem to point to a far greater societal psychological depression than was experienced during the "Great Depression" of the Twenties. Instead of getting into the swim of things, countless people now prefer to float through life on a raft of apathy.

We have encountered stress from so many directions that a large segment of the population has been numbed into a state of indifference, a state of vegetation and docile compliance. These people go through many of their routines with little physical and emotional expression, much like animals in a zoo. Their only stimulation comes artificially from a bottle or pill.

Oddly, some of the fiercest and most formidable animals in the wild, such as the lion, tiger, and bear, eventually become some of the most docile and lethargic animals in the zoo, while many of the traditionally reserved animals become wary and agitated, and often remain so. People are the same. Strong individuals who constantly challenge insurmountable barriers to their urges, wishes, or desires are some of the first to reach a state of apathy. The harder and more often you bang your head against the wall the quicker you may reach a state of unconsciousness (apathy). The lesson to be learned is that instead of banging our heads against the wall, we can find a way around it. It's less painful that way, and it preserves our sanity and ambition.

Destroyers of Life and Love:

Level 1   Anxiety
Level 2   Anger
Level 3   Apathy

The three great destroyers of life and love are what I call the *Negative Triple "A"s*: *Anxiety*, *Anger*, and *Apathy*. Real or perceived threats to our existence result in anxiety (level one); anxiety causes anger and aggressive behavior (level two); and prolonged anger or stress leads to the lowest level, apathy—or depression. It is difficult to escape from a state of apathy. Sometimes a person has to hit rock bottom, or encounter a severe emotional shock, such as a divorce, death of a loved one, a serious illness, or physical trauma, to snap out of it. For some, a spiritual awakening or religious conversion provides relief.

Regardless of what puts us on the road to recovery, we have to make a conscious decision to take control of our lives. Some people interpret this thought process as a submission to a higher power, yet it may be no more than letting go of our resistance to change. To affect positive changes in our lives we first of all have to acknowledge that we have— or are part of—a problem. Then we must discover the root of the problem, set realistic goals, and write a personal mission statement to define our priorities and objectives in life.

These principles are the basis for all successful 12-step recovery programs for addictive behavior. The theme of these programs, which must be present in our personal programs as well, is that *we must be strong enough to admit we are weak*, and that we need help from others on our journey to recovery.

By taking control of our lives—one day at a time—through *knowledge* and *experience*, we can insulate ourselves from the chaos surrounding us and enjoy a good life. As we balance our urges and the behaviors associated with their gratification, gain control over anxiety, let go of our obsessions and compulsions, our behavior and the behavior of those around us will bear a semblance of normalcy. With this accomplished we can experience true happiness, satisfying relationships, and a much deserved inner peace.

Eat, Drink, And Be Married

7

Though anxiety is our worst enemy, there are times when a bit of it is necessary. It serves as a warning system, causing us to be wary in potentially harmful circumstances. It prepares us to run when our senses conclude that a threat is too great to be overcome. It also helps to assure satisfaction of our basic needs by creating a sense of urgency, such as when we are hungry, thirsty, or have other bodily needs. While high levels of anxiety can lead to illness, mild, intermittent stresses boost the immune system.

Fear motivates us to work, to be successful, and to protect our family and possessions (fight). It sets our priorities, often making them different from our mate's. It also makes biological clocks tick louder (fuck + feed).

Since the *fight* and *flight* urges are defensive measures, or secondary responses, while the *feed* and *fuck* urges are sustaining or primary measures, it is not so surprising to find that our difficulties in life and love originate in the *feed* and *fuck* departments. We obviously encounter major struggles in all four dimensions of our lives, but most of our anxiety stems from real or perceived threats to these two basic urges—our security and pleasure. We can depict our basic urges and subsequent reactions as follows:

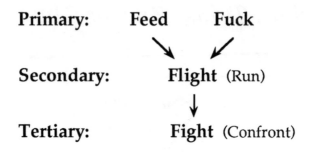

Primary: **Feed**   **Fuck**

Secondary: **Flight** (Run)

Tertiary: **Fight** (Confront)

Our primary concerns are for our security and pleasure, including our ability to reproduce ourselves, which is nature's primary concern. We may believe that we are more concerned about our mate's happiness and pleasure than our own, but what we personally consider altruism and regard for another is often merely an effort to assure the longevity of the relationship so that *we* can ultimately obtain security and pleasure.

Sometimes we cater to our mate's needs to preserve the security of the family for the sake of our children. Since our children are our tie to immortality, their well-being often takes precedence over our own. The only other reason we may allow someone else's needs to come first is the belief that perhaps by subordinating our desires and pleasures to those of another we will inherit a better life in the hereafter.

When we encounter real or perceived threats to the security and pleasure aspects of our lives we begin to experience anxiety (flight). At that point we have four choices:

1. We can run away or escape from the threat (flight);

2. We can stay and confront it (fight);

3. We can remain uncertain and do nothing, which, leaves us in a state of anxiety (flight); or,

4. We can ignore the situation (apathy).

The ideal choice is to confront the situation and devise a positive plan to eliminate the source of the anxiety. Running away just allows matters to worsen and often leaves us feeling guilty. Of course, there are times when running away is necessary: to protect ourselves or to find some happiness. But when we are committed to remaining with someone, we must refine our ability to handle the inevitable moments of conflict.

As discussed, when a situation cannot be altered, and it's not life-threatening, the best thing we can do is change our attitude about it. This helps to preserve our health and sanity. Since many of the little irritating aspects of a relationship are not worth fooling with, try to forget about them. Focusing on the minor issues destroys, rather than improves, a relationship.

When men and women choose a mate, their primary concerns are appearance (fuck), companionship (feed), security (feed), sexual pleasure (fuck), and procreation (fuck). Therefore, **the cancer that destroys a relationship originates within the *feed* and/or *fuck* departments**. Although most women want to mate with a successful man (fight), their primary goal is to have security (feed) and close companionship (feed). The attraction to a successful man merely stems from his greater ability to provide security (feed).

If we reconsider Dr. Farrell's conclusion that men work primarily to obtain more and better sex, *fuck* appears to be men's primary urge in life—which many women have been proclaiming all along. The primary urge has simply displaced into the *fight* urge (work/success/hero) in order to improve the chances of being gratified. For most women, the *feed* urge (security/companionship) has displaced into the *fuck* urge (appearance/sexual favors) to, likewise, better the chances of gratification.

Work (fight) is a means to survival, providing money that can be used to purchase food, water, shelter, and clothing. Therefore, a desire to work is ultimately motivated by fear (flight)—a fear of not having the necessities. In all species, survival of the fittest is the rule, and aggression (fight) is often the method used to establish or maintain rank and territory. Therefore, our biology compels us to strive for higher status on the socioeconomic scale to better our chances of survival. This is nature's version of social security.

We may think we choose to work for noble reasons, but we are really only striving to improve our chances of satisfying our *feed* and *fuck* urges. For men, that translates into gaining access to better women (providing security in exchange for sex). For women it means access to better men (sex in exchange for security).

Men become anxious and frustrated in their attempts to be successful at *fight* (work, sports, hero, etc.) and often express anger and other inappropriate behavior toward their mates. At first glance, men appear to be obsessed with outdoing their peers. But the true motivator, beyond obtaining basic needs, is competition for women (fuck).

Women become anxious and frustrated in their attempts to find and maintain close companionship with a successful man and, consequently, develop a tendency to fret over real or perceived deficits in their attractiveness and levels of intimacy. Men become obsessed with success; women become obsessed with improving their appearance.

The *feed* category of our lives includes eating, drinking, elimination, socializing, companionship, home, security, dependence, female bonding, motherhood, and non-sexual affection. Of these, eating, drinking, companionship, security, dependence, and non-sexual affection are more likely to be sources of conflict between men and women.

Research has shown that poor diet can cause such things as depression, anxiety, insomnia, dementia, hallucinations, personality changes, irritability, hyperactivity, restlessness, nightmares, and teeth grinding. So, the first effort to improve a relationship should begin in the kitchen. By assuring that your mate gets proper nutrition, his chances of developing behavioral problems from a poor diet will be minimized. Vitamin supplementation may also be of help.

Carbohydrates produce serotonin, a calming neurochemical, while protein produces dopamine and norepinephrine, which cause alertness. Research has shown that norepinephrine is associated more with anger, epinephrine with fear. This explains why we crave certain foods depending upon our mood. By applying this knowledge in food planning you can influence your mate's behavior to some degree. If he's agitated and upset, give him dessert. If he's lethargic and apathetic, offer him protein. It is not by accident that many business deals close over lunch, or new relationships are launched over dinner. The old adage, "The way to a man's heart [or pocketbook] is through his stomach" is not so far off after all.

Proper elimination is conducive to good behavior. While some may find discussion of personal body functions unpleasant, knowing that a mate is irritable because of constipation or diarrhea can foster compassion instead of animosity.

We learn early in life to repress our natural urges to urinate and defecate through potty training. Unfortunately, delaying the elimination of bodily wastes causes anxiety, which leads to poor behavior. While we cannot revert to the old method of relieving ourselves behind the nearest bush, we *can* learn to respond quicker when nature calls.

Eating and drinking disorders facilitate the dissolution of many relationships, but in most cases these conditions are merely secondary responses—displacement activities or coping mechanisms—arising from personal or interpersonal conflict (anxiety). Though the underlying anxiety may have originated in childhood or a previous relationship, it can be influenced—for better or for worse—by the dynamics of a current relationship.

Of course, some people are genetically predisposed to eating disorders, alcoholism, or drug addiction and may continue those behaviors in spite of their mate's best efforts to improve the relationship. Still, most addictive behaviors are affected by the status of the mating game.

People leaving relationships because of a partner's food, alcohol or drug problem usually report that the *increasing dependency* and *decreasing companionship* (feed) drove them away. This means that the primary cause of male-female friction in the *feed* category originates in the companionship, security, dependence, and/or non-sexual affection departments.

Since sex is the male's primary concern, and security and intimacy are the female's primary concerns, we can safely conclude that most male-female relationships end because of *deficiencies* in those areas. Let's narrow this down a little more.

Putting Up With The Bull

8

Since extensive research shows human and animal behaviors to be comparable, including mating rituals, I decided to take a field trip to a farm and observe the animals. I knew that animals have the same four basic urges of *fight, flight, feed,* and *fuck,* as humans do. But I wanted to know more about the primary behaviors of *feed* and *fuck,* since the *fight* and *flight* urges merely represent secondary reactions—reactions to a real or perceived threat to *feed* or *fuck.*

While driving out to the country I reflected upon my own life. I had experienced both good and bad times through the years, but I didn't seem to be getting any happier on my journey to maturity. This was inconsistent with what I had assumed to be the natural order of things. Why did I feel so good at times, yet so unexplainably insecure and lonely at others?

With my background in science, I reasoned that it was hormone, neurotransmitter, or perhaps blood sugar fluctuations—or maybe even the phase of the moon. Yet there did appear to be a certain set of circumstances that, when encountered, caused me to feel that life was worthwhile and stimulating. I was reasonably sure that those circumstances were consistent and gender-specific.

I concluded that whatever generally satisfied and stimulated the male was occupational/sexual in nature, and whatever satisfied and stimulated the female was more companionship/appearance in nature. It was obvious that a positive outlook on life coincides with a good self-image for both sexes, and a good self-image is largely dependent upon the levels of gratification of our basic urges or desires, which are highly influenced by the emphases and expectations we place upon them.

Men have a better self-image when they are happy with work and sex; women have a better self-image when they are happy with their appearance, their personal relationships, and their ability to be a good mother.

As I was mulling this over in my mind, I spotted a farm with cows, horses, pigs, and sheep. As I neared the house, I spotted the farmer out by the barn putting feed into a trough. I parked, walked over to him and introduced myself. I told him I enjoyed animals and would like to look around. He appeared hesitant at first, but then agreed, and I offered to follow him around on his chores.

We eventually came to a corral where a cow and bull shared a fenced area.

"Are you trying to breed them?" I asked.

The farmer nodded a quiet yes, and I watched as the bull attempted to mount the skittish cow without much success. She kept moving about to prevent him from entering her.

"Looks like he's going to need some help," I said.

"Oh, she'll give in pretty soon," he replied. "She puts him off awhile, getting him all worked up and excited, and then she lets him have it."

Memories of my youth flashed through my mind. I remembered how I had pursued a female just like the bull before me, only to be put off time and time again. I remembered getting all worked up. I couldn't sleep, didn't eat much, and I thought about the girl day and night.

My mind turned back to the mating process in animals.

"Do all your other animals go through this pre-coital ritual?" I asked the farmer.

"You mean, do they play hard to get?" he queried.

"Yes," I replied.

"Every animal *I've* ever known acts that way," he said. "I guess it makes it more excitin' for 'em or somethin'."

I shared my thoughts about my teen-age years with my host, who nodded his head in reply. "Yeah, I remember those days," he said. "Them girls sure could get a guy all worked up an' all."

After a pause he added thoughtfully, "But then you get married and that all stops. The women start complainin' all the time, and us men just go off to work every day—and maybe fishin' once in awhile, when they let us."

We kept watching the mating game between the cow and the bull, and I thought about the farmer's comments. Other than not always being happy about going to school or meeting my parents' curfew on Saturday nights, growing up really wasn't all that bad. In fact, it was thrilling at times, especially when I was doing something I really enjoyed, like participating in sports or chasing a special girl. After marriage and settling down, however, life began to turn somewhat mundane and routine.

"Well, he made it," the farmer said suddenly, interrupting my thought and focusing me again on the mating taking place before us.

The bull had succeeded in his effort to mate with the cow and she was allowing him to enjoy the fruits of his labor. This coupling continued for a few minutes and then, without warning, the cow suddenly pulled away and ran to the opposite side of the corral.

"What happened?" I asked the farmer.

"Oh, nothing," he replied. "She knew he had done his thing, and it was time to get away from him again."

I recalled how our family dog had behaved similarly toward the neighbors' dog when he tried to mate with her. The male would chase her around the yard and she would play hard to get. When she became too tired to put up any more resistance, she would give in and allow mating to occur. A short time later our dog would suddenly attempt to escape, just as the cow had done, dragging the male dog howling along until they could separate. Then, our dog would scurry off and hide from him.

I quickly compared the animals' behavior to that of humans, and I remembered how difficult it was to succeed with a girl, and how that amplified the desire and passion, often becoming an obsession. The farmer was right when he commented on how the glow and passion fade after a few years together, how the intensity of the relationship diminishes as the couple focus on other aspects of living.

In my own life the level of excitement experienced at the beginning of marriage had somewhat waned over time with just occasional reminders of the earlier passion. I realized that this observance was universal with couples I knew, and that I was uncovering an important link in the chain of events that eventually destroys a relationship between a man and a woman.

I would have to think this out. I thanked the farmer for allowing me to visit, and I headed home, leaving behind the animals that behaved just like people.

That night, I awoke from a dead sleep and sat straight up in bed.

"That's it!" I exclaimed aloud. "The missing piece to the puzzle!"

My heart was pounding, my thoughts raced, my muscles tensed, and I began to feel tingling all over my body as if my primitive instincts were acknowledging the discovery of something that had imprisoned man for perhaps thousands of years. It was suddenly clear to me that the *social diseases* we had all come to know too well were simply by-products of man's captivity—much like the problems experienced by the animals behind the confining bars in a zoo!

I realized what true happiness is. *True happiness is being yourself in your natural habitat.*

Then I realized what the self is. *Self is the total of our biological urges, modified to varying degrees by any conditioning we have obtained from our environment.*

Immediately, I knew I didn't like my current *self* and I decided from that point on I would peel off my shell, break off the shackles that I had placed upon myself, and find out who I really am.

I now understood loneliness. *Loneliness is not being truly happy.* Yet, loneliness is a normal feeling when experiencing the loss of a loved one, due to the abrupt severing of the bond that existed between two people. Loneliness can even be experienced when you are with someone, especially when they no longer satisfy your basic urges or needs.

On and on the truth began to unfold. I saw that we were given some directions and encouragement at times as we trodded our twisted path to destruction. We were told that: "The truth shall set you free," that "We hold these truths to be self-evident," and that the important things are "life, liberty, and the pursuit of happiness." But alas, our chains were making too much noise and we couldn't hear the message. Not only that, we were also blind and couldn't see the truth that had been around us all the while—*the truth we needed to escape from our bondage.*

I realized that when children judge their parents crazy and mixed-up, they are correct. The children know something is wrong but can't identify what it is. Unfortunately, these children—conditioned by their confused parents—

eventually become mixed-up grown-ups themselves.

I also understood that we must teach children respect for themselves and others at an early age, and reinforce these truths as they grow into adults by good parental examples. I knew that children could be happy and creative—being themselves in their natural habitat—once the adults were positive role models.

Now it was clear to me why I had felt insecure and frustrated at times in my life. I also understood why married men and women become attracted to someone new, and why they usually encounter the same problems no matter who their partners are.

I could see that true friendship and regard for one another comes from a bonding of our *selves*, and that respect for myself comes from simply being my*self*. I began to think how foolish we had been, looking for answers we already possessed but had failed to notice. Emerson said it a long time ago: *"Though we travel the world over to find the beautiful, we must carry it with us, or we find it not."*

I realized that disease doesn't come from without, it comes from within; that we bring diseases upon ourselves and suffer the consequences of our behavior with increasing severity.

I saw the world unfold before me and realized that unhappy, frustrated men and women were causing the turmoil on our innocent planet. I saw that our forefathers had escaped one form of bondage by coming to this land, but along with them came unhappy and confused individuals who later bound everyone up again—to an even greater degree. As Sitting Bull, tribal leader of the Teton Sioux, once said of the white man:

> *"We have now to deal with another race—small and feeble when our fathers first met them, but now great and overbearing...The love of pos-*

*session is a disease with them...They claim this
mother of ours, the earth for their own and fence
their neighbors away: they deface her with their
buildings and their refuse..."*

I realized that the greatest battle is not with our brother
but with ourselves; and that we will never improve our environment until we improve ourselves.

I also realized how foolish we had been debating over
where we had come from, instead of figuring out what we
are doing and where we are going. I no longer feared death,
because now, I understood it. I knew that our ultimate reward is to die happy, being our*selves* in our own natural
habitat.

I was thankful that we had not inhabited other worlds.
Imposing our unhappiness and confusion upon other planets
is not the moral thing to do. I did, however, understand
man's desire to escape the filth and confusion he has left on
this earth, yet I grieved at the loss of those who willingly
sacrificed their lives in that attempt. It was clear that we will
never fully appreciate the wonders of the universe until we
remove the tethers that keep our souls bound in turmoil here
on earth.

Finally, I realized that it wasn't going to take a lifetime
to find my*self*. I was born there. I had just made the mistake
of leaving.

Playing (Not Too) Hard To Get

9

Observing the antics of the mating game in the animal world we see that a particular phenomenon occurs as the process unfolds: the female often plays hard to get, and the male becomes maximally stimulated before intercourse occurs. Following coitus the female immediately withdraws from the male, leaving him alone at his most vulnerable moment. In humans, that *moment* is when the male is revealing his true *self* to the female: fulfilling his biological destiny.

Comparing ourselves to the animal world we see the contrast in our lovemaking—where we have failed. The woman lingers in the afterglow only to be burned by it later. Failing to get his pursue switch reset the man becomes discontented and looks elsewhere for a challenge. What is perplexing to the woman is that her mate acts normal and pleasant in his association with others, reserving his moodiness and irritability for her alone. He may not even know why he feels frustrated around her.

The woman, now unpursued and confused, begins to question her attractiveness. Her self-image begins to suffer, and *she* becomes unhappy. *Power plays escalate because of the decreased mutual respect.* Money and other vital issues take on greater significance, and each person begins to criticize the other out of the frustration associated with his or her predicament. Unfortunately, these diseased men and women infect their children and the rest of the world with their destructive behavior and negative attitudes.

It is easy to explain why some men and women become preoccupied and even obsessed with fantasy, pornography, and other vicarious activities. Unfulfilled females read romance novels and watch soap operas depicting the caring, communicative, pursuing male, while unfulfilled men prefer sex movies and porn magazines. In essence, this is our escape from reality. By periodically projecting our imaginations into fantasyland we can temporarily transcend our predicament and obtain a fix to help us get by in our primary-fantasy-deficient real world.

Not surprisingly, men and women rely less on fantasy, pornography, new sexual techniques, sex toys, and other artificial stimulation when the mating game proves to be challenging and passionate. Although fantasy is deemed a healthy endeavor by some experts, it is merely a displacement activity used to compensate for deficits in the relationship—a psychological crutch to keep it going.

Though fantasy *can* help a relationship last a little longer, it does very little to solve the underlying problems. Most fantasies have to be expanded over time to attain the same level of gratification, and the gap between the expected and reality widens, causing further discontent.

Disappointment = Expectations - Reality

To rectify this situation, adequate courting or pre-coital arousal must take place so that the female can surrender exhausted, no longer requiring reassurance of her mate's desire for her after the act. She must understand that over time her lingering is destructive to the relationship. Since the male prefers a challenge, the female's resistance adds to his pleasure and focuses his attention on *her* instead of pornography or another woman. By prolonging the courting or foreplay phase the female not only experiences better communication with her mate, she also increases the likelihood of *her* orgasm. Also, her self-image improves as a result of the extra time spent on courting.

A man usually prefers having his mate climax first so he can suspend worrying about giving her pleasure and begin concentrating on his own experience. If he climaxes prematurely, he may lose his erection, and she may not be adequately stimulated to achieve orgasm. This can be intimidating and ego-crushing for a male. By delaying intercourse through gentle resistance, or playing a little hard to get, a woman can assure and heighten the pleasure for herself and her partner, and generate a perpetual courtship—courtship that is so important for the self-image of both sexes and, ultimately, their individual health and happiness.

Men who experience erectile dysfunction (impotence) may find their problem reinforced when their mates try to help by being extra sexy. Unfortunately, this often causes a vicious circle by creating more performance anxiety. As mentioned earlier, the male derives most of his anxiety from work and sex. If too much anxiety accumulates in either area, creativity and performance become impaired. If, on the other hand, just enough anxiety is present to motivate without impairing, the male rises to the challenge both work and sex present. By withdrawing instead of pursuing, the female takes the pressure off the male and he can relax. This, in turn, allows his sexual urge to reappear from behind the wall of anxiety and resentment, and he can begin to perform normally again.

Men with erectile problems often worry that their mates

are fulfilling their sexual urges elsewhere, which only serves to increase anxiety and frustration. Reassurance of marital fidelity may be necessary sometimes, but not to the point of overdoing it. A little uncertainty adds a bit of spice to life and keeps the flame of passion burning more brightly.

While more females than males suffer from inhibited sexual desire and aversion disorders, many men are becoming apathetic when it comes to having sex with their wives. Impotence is an increasing problem and countless women are frustrated with partners who are sexually lethargic or indifferent. Oddly enough, most of these men frequently think about sex and often own a stash of pornographic material. The problem is not low libido, it's just low interest in a particular person. When a woman becomes critical and demanding, and no longer represents a challenge for her mate, impotence and indifference may surface.

Charlie and Virginia had been married for twenty-two years when Charlie began to experience occasional impotence. Although Virginia had started out with a low libido, she eventually became more interested in sex. But her attempts to spice up their sex life were either futile or short-lived, and the accumulated tension caused her to have neck and shoulder pain. That's when she came to see me.

After diagnosing muscle tension, I asked if she had any significant sources of stress. She revealed the sexual problems. Charlie had slowly lost interest in sex over the last ten years and now was content with an evening of television, often retiring to bed at an early hour. This kind of lifestyle left Virginia resentful and frustrated. She even admitted some attraction to a man she met at a bowling alley. But she wanted to preserve her marriage and was open to suggestions, so I gave her some simple advice.

86

Virginia's first task was to search the house and garage to see if Charlie was hiding pornographic materials. If she found his stash, it would suggest that he was still interested in sex and simply needed some help perceiving Virginia as a desirable woman again. She had to understand that even though a man may find his mate desirable, certain vicarious activities may still be practiced simply for their stimulating and tension-relieving value. If a particular sexual habit developed at a young age, eliminating it altogether may be difficult or even impossible. Moreover, attempting to eliminate it may cause other problems to surface.

Although it required a thorough search, Virginia found Charlie's Playboy magazines, hidden in the garage. She didn't disturb them. Confronting Charlie would only embarrass and alienate him from her even more, as well as reinforce his habit. Virginia felt a little resentful at her discovery, but was glad that Charlie hadn't given up on sex altogether. The fact that he had the magazines was highly suggestive of his ability to achieve an erection and climax.

Virginia suspended all criticizing and demanding, and begin subtly withdrawing from Charlie, since trying to move closer to him only compounded the problem and increased his performance anxiety. She was not cold and insensitive, but became just a little less available and accomodating. This strategy gave her some time to build her self-confidence and self-esteem by completing a few projects that she had been putting off—one of which was taking a self-improvement course at the community college. Charlie was a bit agitated and puzzled at first by Virginia's distancing, but he ultimately was drawn to her by the resulting tension placed upon the bond between them, and he began to communicate more readily.

The net effect of Virginia's distancing was to increase Charlie's awareness of the problem and his receptivity to solutions. Once he showed renewed interest in her, Virginia asked him to answer the *Ten-Question-naire*. His answers helped clarify the areas of their lives and relationship that needed attention. When they came together to set mutual goals and plans for personal achievements, their relationship took on fresh life and blossomed. Charlie's impotence spells became less frequent and their sex life returned to a satisfactory level. Charlie didn't throw away his magazines, but his interest in them diminished substantially.

When a man doesn't have morning erections or fails to respond to pornographic material, a physical examination is in order. Some medications can cause impotence, as can certain health problems, including diabetes and hardening of the arteries. Prolonged stress or depression may be the culprit. One study showed that 50 percent of men and 71 percent of women seeking help for low libido were chronically depressed. Decreased sexual desire has also been linked to PMS.

By simply changing a medication or treating an underlying condition, many cases of impotence and decreased sexual desire can be alleviated. As public awareness on these subjects increases, the stigma associated with them decreases, clearing the way for more men and women to seek help.

$\mathcal{PCW}$

10

$\mathcal{V}$arious experts have noted the bonding effect of the male and female orgasmic experience and indicate that it is a psychologically impressionable event, one that can be taken advantage of for therapeutic purposes.

Steven Naifeh and Gregory White Smith, authors of *Why Can't Men Open Up*, asked a tense, high-strung man if he was "...ever free of the anxiety coiled up inside him? The man thought for a moment, then finally said yes—but *only* for those few brief minutes after orgasm. For those precious moments, he didn't feel the burdens." That observation is supported by sex experts Masters, Johnson, and Kolodny who state: "Psychologically, orgasm is usually a time of pleasure and suspended thought—the mind turns inward to enjoy the personal experience."

Barbara De Angelis, Ph.D., in her book *Sex Secrets About Men Women Should Know,* acknowledges that, "He may be different afterward. Countless women have complained that their husbands are withdrawn after lovemaking. What they don't understand is that men do this to regain control over their emotions...A man I once treated said that lovemaking was the one experience in which he felt totally free to express himself emotionally. But afterward, he felt he had to pull himself together and *get back to being a man.*"

Evidence suggests that the male is more susceptible to mental-sexual programming at the time of orgasm. In their discussion of the treatment of psychosexual disorders, Masters, Johnson, and Kolodny describe the process of "...Orgasmic reconditioning, wherein a person might be instructed to masturbate using his paraphilia fantasy and to switch to a more appropriate fantasy (for example, intercourse with his wife) just at the moment of orgasm."

Sexual arousal is largely under the control of the parasympathetic portion of the autonomic nervous system. When orgasm occurs, however, the nervous system suddenly switches over to the sympathetic side. This sudden shift may explain why we are more susceptible to mental-sexual programming at that point. Also, the level of oxytocin rises during intercourse. In addition to its ability to hasten childbirth and promote lactation, this hormone promotes the social bondings involved in choosing a mate and having offspring. Oxytocin not only increases the attraction between the partners, but it also encourages good parenting habits. Some researchers go as far as to say that oxytocin may influence *most* of our social behavior.

Sympathetic discharges (fight, flight) dramatically increase our sensory awareness and recall of similar situations or events in order to improve our chances of survival. Nature correlated sympathetic activity and increased impressionability for a good reason. She also may have deemed it wise to set the nervous system quickly back to the *protect* mode at orgasm so that the biological investment of conception could be guarded expeditiously. The male's focus and motivation switches to something besides continued, unnecessary (from a biological standpoint) sexual activity. Unfortunately, anxiety can upset this balance, resulting in an over-sexed state that is never fully satisfied.

The female's greater ability to have multiple orgasms suggests that she is not as affected by this parasympathetic-sympathetic shift as is the male. He usually requires more time to become aroused again, and his genitals often remain too sensitive for further stimulation for a longer period. More studies need to be conducted to help us better understand this matter, but what we *do* know can be used to an advantage in strengthening a relationship.

Immediately following his orgasm is a good time to get a man's attention, since his mind is now temporarily freed up. By subtly withdrawing from the male shortly after his release—post-coital withdrawal (PCW)—the female can draw his attention to her again, and, simultaneously, activate his possessive instincts—just like taking a bone away from a dog or a toy from a child. Since the male often does this to the female, she should be able to do likewise. In fact, it is necessary at times to put things back into perspective and to reactivate the game.

With PCW the female turns the male's *pursue* switch back on, and he is left with a desire to be with her again. Her withdrawal may be as simple as leaving the room, or it may be more extreme, such as leaving town or the country.

PCW generates a psychological magnetism that continues to attract the male time and time again. Instead of allowing him to drop into a stage of boredom and apathy from too little challenge or lack of intrigue, he stays interested and involved with his mate. This can be compared to the power exerted by two magnets. As the distance between the magnets decreases, the attractive forces increase until they meet. Then the forces cancel out, and the magnets must be separated again to perceive the energy and attraction between them.

The more obvious and abrupt the female withdrawal, the

greater the potential effect upon the male. This is due to the male's possessive instincts and his unconscious biological urge to assure that *his* sperm has a chance to fertilize the female's ovum before it becomes adulterated by that of another male.

Some males respond readily to PCW while others require more of a jolt. The strongest and most impressionable effect of a female's withdrawal occurs when executed somewhere near the peak of the male's orgasm. But if a female withdraws *before* the male has reached his climax, she may cause him to experience physical and psychological insult, and he may express his dissatisfaction through anger and aggression (fight). Of course, withdrawing during coitus is classified as *coitus interruptus* instead of post-coital withdrawal.

A female performing coitus interruptus could certainly get a male's attention or perhaps get even with him over some previous disagreement. But few men appreciate a woman who leaves them at this vulnerable moment, and the relationship may be damaged. The key is to withdraw just enough to activate his possessive instincts—to protect his biological and social investment—without pushing him to aggression. It is best to start with a small dose of PCW and gradually increase to the point that the desired results occur. It sometimes takes a little while for a response, so be patient.

Of course, post-coital withdrawal only works when the male is physically and mentally capable of responding. And, obviously, he must be attracted or bonded to the female to some degree. A male no longer committed to the relationship may simply appreciate this separation and channel his energies into his career or other endeavors, including, pursuing another woman. Yet, playing this game can offer the female an indication of how committed a man is to the relationship. As my grandmother used to say, "By moving the cookie jar a little higher on the shelf, you can discover how determined he is to have the cookie."

Considering that the male is right-brain oriented—visual-spatial, sexual, figuring out mazes, etc.—it is easy to understand how the female's escape affects him. He sees her leave (visual), he becomes spatially oriented to her absence, he remembers just having had intercourse with her, and now he is trying to figure out why she left or how he can capture her again. This parallels the behavior of cats as they play with a mouse by alternately subduing it and letting it go, or a dog repeatedly fetching a stick—perpetuation of the game that stimulates them (the fight/pursue urge).

This may sound calculated and manipulative, but this is the very root of the malady in most male-female relationships. One would think that as intellectually advanced as we are, we would be beyond this type of behavior. But we are not. Just as with animals, when the game has lost its flavor or the prize is too difficult to attain, the tendency is to retire from the game and move on to other matters: a priority shift. Consequently, women must help men keep courtship a priority through subtle motivation.

The motivational power of anxiety was demonstrated in the classic experiment in which a group of men were greeted by an attractive woman immediately after they crossed a narrow bridge strung over a deep gorge. These men rated the woman significantly more attractive and felt more aroused by her than did another group of men who met the same woman under less-stressful conditions.

Perhaps this is why our mate often finds us less attractive as the relationship settles in. Since our first encounters usually entail some level of anxiety and passion, our initial perceptions may be overinflated. The old saying that "love is blind" is incorrect. Love is *not* blind, since it often sees more than what's really there.

This phenomenon helps to explain why PCW can be so effective. Paradoxically, a woman gradually becomes invisible to her mate when she is constantly visible. By periodically withdrawing she creates a little anxiety and mystery that serves to arouse her mate and increase his perception of her attractiveness, as well as prevent him from taking her for granted.

This brings up the age-old question of why it is the woman's responsibility to keep the fires burning? Why can't men just continue doing the things they did during the courtship?

The primary reason is that men are task oriented. During the initial stages of a relationship the male puts forth substantial effort to gain access to the woman and win her favor. But once he has her affections, he moves on to something— or someone else—more challenging and stimulating. If the female fails to reactivate the game by withdrawing, the relationship may dissolve because of the *male's* distancing.

In the words of Drs. Connell Cowan and Melvin Kinder, authors of *Women Men Love, Women Men Leave*: "Some of you may be saying, 'Well, all this sounds like game-playing, and I don't want to have to do that.' You are right—it *is* a game, and, when played with sensitivity, a delightful one for both women and men. But 'game' does not mean manipulation. While understanding, partnership, and friendship are dimensions of a relationship that do not involve strategy, passion is and always has been a game. Arousing and sustaining romance and passion in a man requires understanding how men operate and being willing to put your knowledge into action. You may choose not to play the game, but you will be missing out on a lot of enjoyment and fulfillment."

It is interesting to see the intrigue and curiosity generated in a male by a somewhat elusive female. Most men seem attracted to this type of woman and often go to great lengths to associate with her, though she may not be exceptionally attractive.

94

According to Frederick Humphrey, past president of the American Association For Marriage And Family Therapy, women are beginning to play hard to get again. They are finding that their aloof approach pays off when dealing with men. Humphrey says that most men prefer a challenge and are turned off by women who are too eager and readily accessible. A gentle resistance draws males further into a relationship. Several studies have shown that most men prefer courting a somewhat hard to get yet receptive woman.

This helps to explain why budding relationships fare better when the *female* gets up and leaves following intercourse—or the morning after—instead of the male departing. Her leaving draws him toward her again as opposed to remaining and causing him to feel as if he must escape the closeness. Perhaps the old custom of partners keeping separate sleeping quarters was not such a bad idea after all.

Desire inherently denotes a lack of something or a longing. In other words: DESIRE = WANT − HAVE. For how can you desire something if you already (or always) have it? Therefore, PASSION = FRUSTRATED DESIRE. To create passion and desire, a real or perceived deficit must be present. Remember, the formula for anxiety equals WANT − HAVE, which is the same formula for desire. Therefore, DESIRE = ANXIETY. Passion and desire arise from the anxiety associated with physical and/or emotional distancing, not closeness. The pleasurable and satisfying feeling of closeness actually signifies the end of the passion cycle, since we now have what we desired.

Desire arises from a real or perceived threat of losing our mate or the benefits of the relationship, such as sexual pleasure (fuck), security (feed), social standing (fight), and a means of having offspring (fuck). To maintain desire in a relationship the female must periodically create a real or perceived loss of consortium through subtle distancing.

The thrill and excitement of a new love stems from the

anxiety associated with overcoming the barriers to sex and the fear of rejection. Once these barriers disappear, the thrill and excitement diminish—sometimes rapidly. Unable to identify the source of this change, each person becomes frustrated and resentful, and starts criticizing some of the more obvious flaws in the relationship.

According to William Betcher, M.D., author of *Intimate Play: Creating Romance In Everyday Life,* "Romanticism is often associated with frustrated desire. We seem to need barriers, if not unattainability, in order to kindle passion…I'm convinced that we have to reckon with our need for keeping a certain distance and find healthy ways of preserving mystery and secrecy in spite of familiarity. Our genitals and our psyches are inextricably linked by the seductive thread of taboo."

There is a reason we are this way. The basic rift between men and women has arisen as a result of deviation from the ideal mode of male-female sexual interaction, augmented to a great degree by the anxiety arising from both sexes assuming roles that differ from those conditioned over thousands of years as hunter-gatherers. Culture outpaced biology to such an extent that man was no longer afforded the luxury of expressing his urges in direct, traditional fashions, and suppression and repression came into play.

As man moved away from his original identity and became involved in diverse lifestyles and occupations, previously focused and demarcated urges blurred and overlapped, resulting in a level of inner confusion and inappropriate behavior when encountering conflict and anxiety. Consequently, much of modern man's anxiety is intangible and unfounded, and difficult to identify and dispel.

According to Patrick Carnes, Ph.D., author of *Out of the Shadows: Understanding Sexual Addiction,* "It is the pursuit, the hunt, the search, the suspense heightened by the unusual, the stolen, the forbidden, the illicit which are intoxicating to the sexual addict. The new conquest of the hustler, the score of the exposer, voyeur, or rapist, or the temptation of breaking the taboo of sex with one's own child—in essence, they are variations of a theme: courtship gone awry."

Sexual addiction, domestic violence, date rape, and most other social ills are manifestations of repression and the subsequent overlap of the basic urges. As discussed earlier, the repressed hunting instinct (fight/pursue/conquer) boils over into the sexual urge (fuck), and sexual violence or incest occurs. Although the reward or gratification comes largely from the *control* factor (fight), or overcoming the barriers or taboo (flight), the act itself is perpetrated through the sexual urge (fuck).

This very phenomenon occurs on a smaller scale in a relationship when a man withdraws and becomes moody. His urge to pursue gets repressed—which he may not even realize—as a result of the constraints associated with marriage or cohabitation. He then channels his energies or urges into other aspects of his life. If the ensuing displacement activities are benign, society may not suffer. But if they are malignant, everyone pays.

Until her migration into the work force the female maintained a precise and consistent identity as a mother and homemaker. Her role-related anxiety is a somewhat recent issue. The male, on the other hand, has been moving away from his natural role for some time and tends to be more temperamental and less satisfied than the female—although she is becoming more like him all the time. He is still being driven by his innate urges to be a provider and impregnator, and as these two powerful instincts combine, becoming excessive and compulsive, they lead to increased anxiety and an early death. The only significant reprieve males and females get from their confusion and anxiety is when they act in concert with their primitive roles.

In the past, the extended absences associated with the

hunt fanned a couple's desire for each other, and the male's return was celebrated with good cheer and heightened passion. As a result, relationships were reinforced and the family unit grew stronger. Today, relationships rarely encounter extended absences and uncertainty regarding the return of a mate—except perhaps in time of war—and the constant association of the partners easily leads to staleness and discontent. The resulting lack of challenge and adventure causes the male to become irritable and moody. He begins blaming the female for his troubles, starts criticizing her extensively, even abusing her as well as the children. Then he engages in an affair, or becomes an alcoholic, workaholic, or a sportsaholic. He may even resort to suicide as a means of escape. Confused and depressed from the lack of attention the female loses her identity and self-esteem, becomes insecure and anxious, and ultimately resorts to drugs, alcohol, a psychiatrist, another man, or suicide in an attempt to find a solution herself. This is not a pretty picture.

Ironically, most females are working harder than necessary on their relationships and don't realize they can improve things not by *giving* more, but by *withholding* and doing less. As Marcel Proust said, "An absence, the decline of a dinner invitation, an unintentional coldness, can accomplish more than all the cosmetics and beautiful dresses in the world."

When a relationship begins to deteriorate and the male withdraws and clams up, most women do the wrong thing: they pursue the male, mostly out of insecurity, trying to get him to open up and be intimate. This only drives him further away, like a wild animal about to be captured. With implementation of post-coital withdrawal strategy, however, some amazing results can occur for those women willing to try it. This maneuver has reactivated many relationships that had become stagnant and were headed for failure, drawing distant men back into the game and making it more challenging and rewarding for both partners. "Healthy distance is the best method of recapturing intimacy that I know of," says Dean Delis, Ph.D., author of *The Passion Paradox.*

According to Cowan and Kinder:

> "If a man is given too much sex for too long a time, he gradually will tend to become complacent, lose contact with his feelings of passion, even take the woman's desire for him for granted. It's not that he doesn't appreciate or value this gift of love, it's just that when it's given too much, the man loses the excitement attached to it and comes simply to expect it...Don't be afraid to create a little suspense and intrigue...Don't be available all the time. Let him wonder about your love and desire for him occasionally. This won't endanger your relationship, it will cause him to be more respectful, attentive, and interested."

According to the findings of Dr. Anthony Reading, men's perception of how much sex they are getting is about 30 percent less than what they are actually getting. Their underestimation stems from the fact that they always want more. But as Winona Ryder said in the movie *Welcome Home Roxie Carmichael,* "It's good to want things."

Men don't hold exclusive rights to feeling moody and emotionally suffocated. Some women may need to escape from the closeness of a relationship from time to time as well. While men have long been labeled the distancers, women's growing independence and the subsequent threat to the traditional male bastions is generating more and more insecure males. This leaves many women in uncomfortably close and dependent relationships from which they would like to escape. They may even have affairs with men who are less dependent, parallelling men's traditional behavior of having affairs with less-dependent women.

If a woman withdraws at the same time her mate feels especially insecure, the relationship suffers—just as it does when the reverse occurs. Still, the solution is the same. When a man begins to sense that his mate feels smothered and is becoming distant, he can usually improve things by withdrawing and giving his partner some time and space to move back into the relationship on her own free will. It takes emotional strength to withdraw when the natural tendency is to move closer. Yet moving closer just drives the other person further away.

The dynamics of a male-female relationship—or any relationship—should imitate the elliptical path of celestial bodies: coming in close and then moving away. Time and space allow for relativity and perspective. Although coordinating a pattern of closeness and withdrawal to the mutual satisfaction of both partners can be challenging, it is necessary for building a strong relationship.

Once post-coital withdrawal becomes a legacy and is passed down from mother to daughter, the overall success rate of male-female relationships will improve dramatically, as will our social ills. Despite what some might say, sex is best experienced like the great upheavals of nature: a crescendo of energy to a climax, then a quick withdrawal into herself, leaving man a little more respectful and anticipatory of her return.

The compulsive sexual activity so prevalent in society today is merely an addictive displacement measure used to assuage the anxiety stemming from a real or perceived threat to our existence. Humans or animals in captivity or under stress become violent, oversexed, engage in high levels of masturbation, overeat, and often resort to masochism (nail-biting, hair-pulling, picking at sores, etc.) as they attempt to cope with their predicament. Activation of the pleasure systems associated with these activities provide both stimulation and anesthesia while urges are being repressed in a restrictive or sterile environment. Under normal, non-stressful conditions, sexual activity and other habits are more sporadic and less compulsive, undoubtedly more like nature intended things to be.

If a relationship is progressing along satisfactorily, it is best not to make any changes at that point—*If it ain't broke, don't fix it!* Post-coital withdrawal is a tactic to be respected and used only when a relationship requires specific help. The quiet period immediately following intercourse can be a special time, and there is nothing wrong with extending this post-coital closeness, as long as the relationship is going smoothly. But when the male begins to withdraw and becomes moody or silent, post-coital withdrawal may be necessary to restore the passion and desire of a dying romance, and to improve communication.

I would like to take a moment here and lay the communication myth to rest, once and for all. Many people believe that good communication is important for maintaining a healthy relationship. Yet, as stated by Herb Goldberg, Ph.D., in his book *The New Male-Female Relationship*, "Good communication...emerges as a natural by-product of a balanced interaction, while poor communication is the result rather than the cause of a destructive, unbalanced relationship."

In other words, we are constantly communicating something to our partner, whether it is in a verbal or non-verbal manner. What we usually consider *good* communication is simply hearing what we want to hear, or getting affirmation of our own opinions. When this doesn't occur, we deem the communication *poor*.

Close analysis of the courtship period of a relationship may reveal that communication was not any better at that time than it was after marriage. The difference is that things said during the courtship were uttered while experiencing passion and desire. Certain comments or teasing could be made without having the same destructive effect as after marriage or cohabitation. This reinforces the idea that it's not so much *what* is said as it is the circumstances under *which* it is said.

As a gentleman in one of my male-female communication workshops stated, "Women complain that men don't open up and communicate very well; but when we do, they usually don't like what they hear."

I have heard this comment from men on more than one occasion, and I'm convinced that merely getting someone to open up and spill their guts does not assure a better relationship. What men and women truly want to hear is gender-specific and consistent with their primary fantasies. A woman wants to hear how much she is loved and appreciated, and that she is attractive. She likes being told she is intelligent, but she would rather hear that she is beautiful. What a man wants to hear is that he is a good provider and lover. He likes being told he is handsome and intelligent, but he would gladly trade praise for what's between his ears for praise of what's between his legs.

If we truly want healthy communication, it is necessary to maintain a balanced interaction through shared interests and mutual satisfaction of our basic urges. If we share basic needs and common goals with someone, good communication follows. If, on the other hand, we have little in common or can satisfy our urges elsewhere, communication will be scant.

Communication should be judged by its quality instead of quantity. Babbling about anything and everything is just as annoying as silence. Someone married to a babbler may have coined the phrase, "Silence is golden."

During the courtship period a man seems to have little trouble communicating. After marriage, however, he withdraws into his shell and becomes distant and moody. Since the challenge of the chase is gone and the female is now in his possession, why should he keep pursuing her? A woman might say, "To *keep* her, that's why!" But a man doesn't see it that way, especially if he doesn't perceive it to be a threat. If a woman periodically removes herself from her mate through post-coital withdrawal and creates some distance (anxiety), his pursue switch is reset, his possessive instincts are activated, and he resumes courting gestures and makes attempts at better communication.

When a person cannot be influenced or motivated simply through education, and he fails to respond out of common courtesy, activating one or more of his basic urges may become necessary to get his attention. By creating a little anxiety, some type of response is usually elicited.

A woman must be selective in her use of PCW. If she creates too much anxiety for her mate, especially after he has had a difficult day at work, the extra effort required to play the game may become too great for him and he may soon tire and, subsequently, retire from the game. Like anyone else, a man needs a safe place to unwind. If it's not his home, he may choose a bar, motel, or another woman's arms.

While men enjoy intrigue and anticipation, they also appreciate some comfort and a little mothering now and then, especially when the inevitable feelings of insecurity and inferiority arise. Acting cold and distant when he is trying to move closer to you can damage the relationship. Save the act of post-coital withdrawal for the times when he is moody, withdrawn, and untouchable.

Frustrated or moody men will eventually come to their senses if left alone for awhile. In fact, they come to their senses quicker when they are ignored than when they are pestered and pursued. And don't blame yourself for your mate's anger or moodiness. Some men are naturally irritable and moody and can become cranky for no apparent reason.

Simply withdraw at those times and find your own activities until his mood passes. Be sure to choose a harmless activity instead of something you know will only infuriate him more.

If you *are* responsible for your mate's cloudy disposition, apologize right away. But if you're not, defend yourself against any false accusations. Avoiding the issue and running off in a fit of passive aggression—which may be his modus operandi—will not solve the problem. The exception to this rule is when he abuses you physically. In that case you must get away from the situation—permanently!

The mating game can be exasperating at times and a woman may question her motives for wanting to marry in the first place. Singlehood does have some advantages, and a woman can disregard the rules associated with preserving a marriage. But sleeping alone every night is not very fun, and activities are so much better when you can share them with a lifelong partner. That's what makes memories and allows you to experience the wonders of a family. Judith Sills, Ph.D., author of *A Fine Romance*, puts it this way: "To be single is to live life on an edge. To be married is to live life in a niche. It is not a trade-off. Married is better."

Much of the confusion and frustration in the mating game stems from a lack of knowledge and experience. So, instead of giving up on men, learn to play the game effectively. Who knows? It may become one of your favorite sports!

The Play-By-Play

11

Laurie and Jim were experiencing a mutual loss of respect and passion in their relationship. The appealing ways of courting had gone out the window, making room for a noticeable lack of desire and consideration. They no longer felt accepted and appreciated.

Oblivious to their own faults and shortcomings, each focused on what the other half of the team was either doing wrong or not doing at all, giving credence to the age-old story: *Unmet needs and expectations elevate the anxiety level, which raises expectations, which forces the couple into adopting defensive attitudes, each vying for control and power.* In order for the relationship to survive, this vicious circle has to be broken.

Many woman have to seek counseling on their own, since men gain most of their validation outside the relationship and rarely notice anything wrong with it—except believing that they married a neurotic woman. But Laurie was able to convince Jim to come along. In separate sessions with them, I explained the four basic urges and their effects on male and female behavior. I explained the emphasis each sex places on these urges and how we erroneously expect our partner to be as concerned as we are about the same issues.

I stressed to Laurie the importance of understanding that men are goal oriented, moving on to other things once they have accomplished what they set out to do. This holds true in the mating game. A man expends much energy and demonstrates higher levels of creativity during the courting period to secure a mate. But after he has won her favor he focuses on being a good provider or hero-figure. He believes this will keep her at his side. *For eons men have tried to be the best man in camp to get the best woman in camp, then worked really hard to stay the best man to keep the best woman.*

Instead of continuing to do the thoughtful, personal things for a woman that originally won her favor, a man focuses on his fear of being beat out by a more powerful male. Consequently, he devotes increasing amounts of energy to gain more power while putting forth less effort to strengthen the relationship. As long as the female is still his possession and remains in proximity, a male in a rocky relationship feels more compelled to go to work—to up his value as a provider—than to stay home and be loving and intimate. When he encounters anxiety in the relationship he reacts through *fight* and works harder at his source of income (power, rank) to feel more secure. When a woman encounters anxiety in the relationship she feels more secure staying home and being intimate (feed), which is the opposite reaction the man experiences. To her, his compulsion with work is inappropriate and inconsiderate. To him, it feels like the best way to prevent her from looking for someone better.

Once Laurie understood this fact about men she regained some assurance. She had always taken Jim's compulsion with work as a sign that he didn't care for her, and that he was putting her low on his list of priorities. She finally realized that working hard and long hours is a man's way of giving to the relationship, and is not intended to be a means of escaping his mate's company nor an attempt to hurt her. Going to work simply makes him feel more secure.

One of the greatest sources of anxiety for early humans was obtaining food (feed). Men, the hunters, became anxious when they had trouble finding adequate food for their families. This anxiety carried over into modern man and expresses itself in a compulsion with work (fight).

I advised Laurie to try a little reverse psychology. When Jim was moody and agitated around home she was to suggest that he go to the office and work a while. Instead of verbally whipping Jim into submitting to her request to come home earlier at night, Laurie encouraged him to spend *more* time at work. This took the pressure off Jim and made his coming home earlier feel like it was his own idea. Once he felt in control of the situation, he was able to act civilly without feeling like he was giving in to her nagging.

Using this tactic is similar to capturing an animal: move aggressively and it runs away; act disinterested and it will return on its own. Remember the old nursery rhyme: "Little Bo Peep had lost her sheep and didn't know where to find them. Leave them alone and they'll come home, wagging their tails behind them."

It would be ideal if the man would be sensitive to his mate's needs and realize when he is neglecting her. Instead, he takes her complaint that he spends too much time at work as a lack of appreciation for his efforts, and he retaliates by staying away even more.

Family therapist David Moultrup, author of *Husbands, Wives, and Lovers* says: "An affair is always an attempt to distance from uncomfortable closeness." Attempting to get closer to a withdrawing mate usually only serves to drive him more quickly into someone else's arms.

Laurie now understood why Jim no longer pursued her. He didn't have to. She was always available, doing things for him he could easily have done for himself. She was his "mother," and that had to change before the relationship could improve. I cautioned Laurie not to quit everything she had been doing for Jim too abruptly, since that could damage the relationship. I advised her to slowly cut back on a few things Jim could do for himself, such as folding his own laundry and taking his plate to the sink after dinner.

A bit unsure, Laurie resisted this suggestion, holding on to the old idea that her value to the relationship came largely from her homemaking ability. She had to understand that Jim did not marry her for her domestic skills, nor would he ever leave her for someone who could set a better table or keep a cleaner house. *Men leave their wives because they are attracted to the challenge of getting into another woman's bed.* They may say they fell for her housekeeping skills or understanding heart, but they actually fell prey to the challenge of the conquest.

I impressed upon Laurie the importance of not taking Jim's moodiness personally, even though he might try to blame her for it. As long as she did not do or say anything that ticked him off, she was not be his scapegoat. His frustration most likely stemmed from the fact that he wasn't feeling the thrill associated with courting a confident, somewhat elusive woman. With this urge repressed, the resulting frustration increased his sexual compulsiveness. When Laurie refused his advances, he felt justified in his self-pity and deluded himself into believing that he deserved someone more exciting—someone who would appreciate him.

This is where post-coital withdrawal comes into play. Placating a man with more sex when he is moody and emotionally abusive is like giving candy to an unruly child. The child quickly learns that being difficult elicits a tasty reward. Likewise, an emotionally or physically-abusive man expects sexual favors following his tirades as a reward for improving his behavior.

Insecure and abusive men usually require a lot of sex. The act temporarily satisfies their need for acceptance and control, and provides them with a way of atoning for their abusive behavior. Sex makes them feel as though they are forgiven for their hurtful actions, or that the female provoked the abuse and is now submitting herself to sex as a way of making up for her wrongdoing.

This volley between abuse and reconciliation becomes an addictive and destructive pattern. If, on the other hand, a female withdraws when her mate becomes moody and abusive, she avoids becoming a reward for his behavior, and he will soon realize that his poor attitude and harmful actions are not getting him anywhere.

Laurie did not have a physically-abusive spouse, but she did have to deal with Jim's occasional emotional battering. I explained to Laurie the principle of post-coital withdrawal and its applications. During those periods when Jim was acting cold and somewhat distant toward her, she was to withdraw from him just after intercourse, quietly leaving him to feel somewhat abandoned and alone. This would reset his pursue switch and he would sense that Laurie needed something more from him.

Her withdrawal would simulate the adolescent dating years, when a romantic evening would end with the female's withdrawal at a time when the male desperately wanted to be with her. The ultimate effect of Laurie's tactics would be to get Jim out of the perfunctory sexual rut he was in and cause him to be more conscious of his role in the relationship.

"It took a little while, but it worked," Laurie commented. "I couldn't believe that such a simple act could make that much difference. After we made love, I would get up and go into the other room to read, or sit in the bathroom for a while with the door locked. I even sat in the dark in the back yard a few times. Jim thought I was going crazy and asked me what was wrong. I just told him, I needed to be by myself for awhile. He was sure he had done something wrong to push me away and, undoubtedly, spent some time trying to figure out what it was.

"I hate to admit it, but I got some satisfaction out of knowing that he was feeling the same way I did at times when he withdrew from *me* and wouldn't tell me what was wrong. He got a taste of his own medicine and didn't like it.

"He began to treat me with more respect and started doing little things for me like he used to, perhaps feeling that if he didn't change his ways he was going to lose me."

When Jim was treating her lovingly and things were going smoothly, Laurie would forego post-coital withdrawal and enjoy the special moments of lying together after love-making. But when Jim become moody and distant, she would subtly withdraw as well. She noticed that his spells didn't last as long. He got the message that it did little good to dump on her—unless his cloudy behavior was legitimate and based on something concrete.

A woman dealing with a withdrawn and distant man might be inclined to withhold sex altogether as punishment for his poor behavior. However, this action could end the re-lationship if sex is the only remaining bond. By providing her mate with pleasure and then distancing herself a woman will cause her mate to sense the separation and loss. This, in turn, will activate his possessive instincts and he will pursue her again.

Laurie also began initiating sex at times when Jim was not preoccupied. She admitted sometimes feeling guilty about not making the first move or trying to initiate sex when she knew Jim was preoccupied and unlikely to respond. Men may be perpetually ready for sex, but they have difficulty doing two things at once. Therefore, a woman can eliminate much frustration from the relationship by timing her advances to coincide with times when her mate is not preoccupied.

Unfortunately, men often make advances at impractical times as well, creating tension and frustration. In this instance a woman will do best by giving a rain check that includes a definite time to be redeemed. Sex is a large part of a relationship, and for one partner to engage in sex only when he or she feels like it represents a double standard. No one should be forced to have sex against his or her will, but to consistently put off a partner is unfair and sure to cause problems.

There may be times when a woman would rather provide manual stimulation to relieve her partner's sexual tension in lieu of intercourse. This should be done in a loving manner without haste and repugnance. Although a number of women complain that they have a partner who frequently refuses their sexual advances, more men seem to voice this concern.

Men often make advances when their partner is too busy or not in the mood, and a refusal may be interpreted as a sign of rejection. To prevent resentment a woman can manually stimulate her partner to climax when she prefers not to engage in intercourse. She can simply say that she is not ready for sex, but she would be glad to do something to ease his tension.

Manual stimulation should not become the rule unless illness, such as AIDS, or other circumstance requires it. Manual stimulation in addition to intercourse is often exciting and may be necessary to help a woman achieve orgasm. But most people prefer intercourse and may seek out someone more accomodating if a partner begins relying too heavily on manual stimulation alone.

Jim's periodic masturbation bothered Laurie a little. It made her feel like he was more interested in the women featured in the sex magazines or videos than he was in her. I assured her that men and women both feel sexual tension at times that is effectively relieved by self-stimulation. There is nothing wrong with it. By discouraging it Laurie would open Jim up to resentment and thoughts of being with other women. She needed to tell him that she understood his need to masturbate, that it was normal, and he could do so in her presence without feeling guilty. She would even help him. With this attitude she would gain his respect (appreciation and admiration) on a very deep and private level. Responding this way would help to make *her* the primary source of his stimulation instead of the women on paper or film.

Laurie chose a time during foreplay one night to discuss this with Jim. As they lay naked on the bed in the dark, Laurie took Jim's hand and cupped it around his erect penis and asked him to begin stroking himself. She moved his hand up and down slowly to get him started. She then took his other hand and placed it between her labia and began guiding it up and down.

Laurie, too, became aroused and noticed a level of lubrication much greater than she had experienced in quite a while. Instead of eventually giving in to intercourse, Laurie had Jim bring them both to climax manually. By doing this she associated her image with masturbation in Jim's mind, replacing the image of some woman from a magazine or video. By periodically repeating this form of lovemaking, Laurie strengthened the sexual bond between them. The solution was not to get Jim to stop masturbating, but to convert the situation into a mutually acceptable endeavor that would strengthen their relationship.

Most women resent the fact that their mates look at other women. Laurie was no exception. Few of these women posed any threat to her, but she still felt uncomfortable when Jim gawked. If she noticed him eyeing a pretty woman she would say something sarcastic like, "Don't step on your tongue," or "Put your eyeballs back in." Jim would mumble something back about her being insecure and that it was no big deal.

Women compete with other women for men, and their primary weapon is their appearance. Consequently, women naturally feel threatened when their mate looks at another woman. But criticizing a man for looking is not going to be a deterrent. Both men and women notice attractive members of the opposite sex, yet this occurs so naturally and inadvertently that they fail to recognize how often they gawk themselves. But being on guard for potential threats to their security, each is acutely aware of the other's gawking.

I urged Laurie to accept the fact that Jim was always going to look at other women, and that she was always going to be bothered by it a little. She should not criticize him or make disparaging comments. Instead she should subtly let Jim know that she is aware of his looking by complimenting some particular feature of the other woman that he has undoubtedly already noticed. By reacting in this manner Laurie would project self-confidence instead of insecurity, and Jim would not become defensive. Just because he looked at another woman didn't mean that he was imagining a life with her.

As Laurie continued to learn about the behavior of men, as well as about her own urges and needs, her self-confidence grew. The more her self-confidence grew, the more Jim became attracted to her. She had to let go of her compulsion to rescue him from his moods and start pursuing her own interests to enrich her life and become a more interesting person.

As Jim began to value Laurie more, his courting gestures increased, he stopped dragging his feet, and he kept up with Laurie. He realized that if he didn't, she would leave him behind.

Laurie admitted that she had a tendency to criticize Jim and often enlisted friends and family members in her crusade to change or reprimand him. She had seen her mother do this to her father, yet she had to admit that her mother did not change her father any more than her own complaining and criticizing changed Jim. I assured Laurie that as Jim's respect for her returned he would be more open to constructive criticism at appropriate times and may even ask for her advice. But as long as he felt threatened or resentful he would remain in his irrational, defensive mode, giving little consideration to her suggestions or complaints.

Laurie agreed to stop being critical and placed her faith in Jim's ability to recognize his own shortcomings. She began treating him more like the man she wanted him to be, instead of like the little boy she loathed. As she backed off, Jim became more rational and objective about his behavior and its effect on their relationship.

Laurie and Jim, like most couples, were struggling with money issues. Since money is a symbol of power and control, it easily becomes a source of conflict and competition. Laurie knew that men's value systems are based on money, and when she felt insecure in her relationship with Jim, she found herself trying to gain control of the finances. By exercising greater control in money matters she eased some of her anxiety and felt somewhat comforted by the fact that Jim was now more dependent upon her. But most men are programmed to vie for financial control and do not appreciate having to ask a mate for their own money. Put in this position a man feels like a little boy begging his mother for spending money. Obviously, this does not foster an intimate relationship.

The money issue becomes even more pronounced when the woman is the bigger wage earner. Since a man's identity and self-esteem are rooted deeply in his ability to be a good provider, his value is compromised when his mate brings home a bigger kill. Although many modern-day men won't readily admit it, they still harbor resentment toward women who earn more than they do. In fact, some business relationships and ventures involving men and women fail because of this factor. A woman earning more than her mate should be aware of the possibility that he may eventually seek out a woman less intimidating, if only in a brief affair.

Statistics show that relationships in which the woman earns more do not last as long as those in which the man earns more. The wise woman bringing home the lion's share of the bacon creates an environment that relays sincere appreciation of her mate's contributions. Too many high-wage-earning women fail to handle this situation properly and then wonder why their relationship is bitter and filled with resentment.

Some men are leeches and remain indefinitely in a relationship with a woman who earns more simply to enjoy the fringe benefits. In such a case, the woman's greater earnings may strengthen the relationship.

Though it may be difficult for a woman to give up some of the control associated with having the higher income, it may be necessary to preserve the relationship. A man is validated by a woman who shows her appreciation for his gifts. Although men enjoy the higher standard of living afforded by having a well-paid mate, they still feel incomplete without a woman who is a little dependent upon their financial contributions.

Shortly after marriage, Jim turned over much of the financial responsibilities to Laurie. She paid the bills and balanced the checkbook. The only problem was that when things got tight and Jim couldn't have what he wanted, she got blamed.

It's not uncommon for a man to turn the fiscal responsibility over to his mate and then expect her to keep plenty of money on hand for everything he needs. While turning over the financial responsibility to his wife is a man's way of sharing his kill, he may go overboard in holding her responsible for financial problems. Though *he* may be the cause of the problem, his pride does not allow him to take responsibility for it—especially if he is already harboring some resentment.

Unless he is totally inept at handling money or is so miserly that no one in the family can have their fair share, a woman may save herself some headaches by letting her husband manage the family budget. When he is the family accountant the bulk of the responsibility falls on his shoulders, and his urge to be the provider for the family is validated. He may prefer simply being the provider without the added responsibility of managing the checkbook. But seeing where the money goes gives him some perspective and causes him to be more practical about his own spending.

A woman should stay abreast of the family finances, knowing where all funds are kept, the amounts on hand, and the total debt. Should she face divorce or the sudden death of her partner, she won't have to scurry around in a state of panic trying to piece together the financial puzzle.

Jim was quite capable of managing the money, so Laurie turned the checkbook over to him. Though it meant giving up some power, it paid dividends to the relationship. To keep things running smoothly a budget was drawn up, and they determined how much each could spend outside of paying the monthly bills. They agreed to discuss significant purchases with each other beforehand so that no misunderstandings and undue financial strain occurred. A realistic savings plan was started to provide for emergencies and special purchases. Like most couples, they were spending most of what they made without considering the future.

I knew many of Jim's complaints about Laurie would subside once she changed her attitude. A positive change in one partner helps to improve the behavior of the other. Since Laurie's lack of self-confidence and failure to distance herself from Jim was causing much of his irritability, the biggest battle had been won. Still, there were things Jim could do to facilitate the recovery of their relationship.

He had to realize that his life was out of balance, and that his urges were lopsided due to stress and repression. He had become a workaholic and a sportsaholic trying to assuage his need for acceptance and recognition, as well as to allay his fears of failure and financial problems. As his compulsion with work and sports grew, his family life shrunk. Although Jim considered his work to be his greatest contribution to the family, he failed to understand that his wife and children did not see it that way. They appreciated him as the provider. But they also needed his time and attention to feel accepted, appreciated, and admired, and to respect him.

I assured Jim that I was not skirting the relationship issues he had complained about in our initial session; however, there were more important things going on in his life that needed immediate attention.

With this approach, Jim was able to see that he was not trapped in a bad relationship with a neurotic woman but, instead, had a disorganized personal life. He began to reflect upon himself, instead of how he was going to fend off the combined assault of his wife and her doctor. Once he realized that I was not a mercenary and that I wanted to help him straighten out his life, he accepted me readily. I didn't have to threaten or intimidate him into accepting my recommendations. I simply bolstered his confidence in me by accepting him as he was and offering to help improve his life. Feeling secure and confident that he would gain from our association, he opened up.

Once Jim gained some understanding of life, he wanted to take control of it and get it into balance. He prioritized his life. And as he did, he became more appreciative of his wife and family. He spent more time with them, and their respect for him grew. By eliminating the underlying causes of his anxiety, his compulsive behaviors diminished, and he was able to devote himself to more important matters. He didn't have to pay several hundred dollars to beat a drum or hug other men at a weekend retreat to get in touch with himself. He just had to have some basic knowledge about the simple urges that make him who and what he is, and the tools to keep anxiety from throwing his life out of balance.

Jim had filled out the *Ten-Question-naire* before coming to see me. His answers reflected a lack of direction in life and highlighted the typical male desire to be Superman and have Superwoman for a wife. Jim's personal goals were fuzzy and he was taking life as it came along. He wanted to be the general manager of the car dealership someday, get out of debt—maybe win the lottery—put away some money for the children's college years, and get his nest egg built up for retirement. But he didn't have a game plan to achieve these goals, other than periodically buying lottery tickets.

I impressed upon Jim the need for some realistic personal goals, as well as a few family goals. I stressed the importance of writing his goals down on paper and keeping them out where they could be readily seen. That way everyone would be reminded of the priorities. Without adequate regimentation of time and effort, non-productive activities quickly take over and use up precious financial and physical resources.

Chores

Getting a husband to do his share of the household chores is a little easier when both husband and wife have jobs. Still, a lot of men drag their feet when it comes to doing what their mother did around the house a generation ago. Jim was no exception.

Laurie worked five days a week as a legal secretary for a five-member law firm, often putting in long hours. With three children at home, ages eight, ten, and twelve, she certainly needed help from her husband. Jim, a sales manager for an auto dealer, worked long hours as well. But instead of pitching in with the housework when he could, he always found other things to do—like working on his boat or motorcycle. Laurie resented the fact that he didn't notice when chores were waiting to be done or that she could use help. She figured that if a man sincerely loved his wife he would automatically be considerate and lend a helping hand. Unfortunately, this is rarely the case.

Women do better than men in assembly-line type work, which came to light during World War II when women worked on production lines. Women have better manual dexterity, a longer attention span for repetitive tasks, and are generally more conscientious about their work. Men are project oriented and don't do well with everyday, routine tasks. They like something they can focus on for a while, accomplish it, and then move on to other things. They're great for washing the car, fixing a leaky faucet, mowing the lawn, or changing a light bulb. But when it comes to doing something tedious and repetitious they quickly lose interest. Men should be given chores with this characteristic in mind.

If a man has a particular project under way he is not likely to drop everything to help with menial chores. He won't appreciate being asked to take out the garbage when he's stuck in an awkward position under the dash of the car. It's not so much that he can't or won't help, it's just that it's the last thing on his mind. A woman who constantly has to ask for help may find it necessary to give her husband a list of things that need to be done. It's just like grocery shopping: a woman can go to the store and remember everything she needs, but a man won't do as well without a list.

Timing is the key to eliciting cooperation from your mate. Asking him to do something after he puts down the newspaper will get better results than asking him while he is engrossed in it. Some women make suggestions or requests when they think of them instead of waiting for an opportune time. Consequently, they compete with their mate's projects for attention and usually end up losing, which causes resentment and frustration.

Once Laurie began timing her requests for help from Jim she felt less resentful, her nagging stopped, and Jim took responsibility for more of the household chores. *The circumstances did not change, but a simple attitude change combined with proper timing yielded the desired response.*

Contrary to what men might believe, housework is good for them. According to a study of 79 couples by John M. Gottman, Ph.D., of the University of Washington, husbands who share household chores with their wives are emotionally and physically healthier than men who don't.

So, learn to play the game to win. When you understand the rules, recognize your mate's idiosyncrasies, and "go with the flow," not only does the relationship blossom but you will see yourself as a knowledgeable, competent, and intelligent woman.

The Senior Olympics

12

Some relationships endure without the sexual component, either by choice or because of a physical impairment. In these cases the *feed* urge (companionship, dependence) becomes the primary bonding agent. Over the years most relationships tend to move away from a focus on sex and begin relying on companionship. This transition allows more time for shared activities, such as travel and hobbies. But there is a down side to the The Golden Years.

Males who were once self-sufficient and in control eventually retire, abdicate their dominant position, and become dependent, passive, and childlike (feed). The wife helps her husband with his grooming and dressing, sees that he's fed, times his medications, and cleans up after him. In essence, she assumes the role of his mother. Unfortunately, this only serves to reinforce his mental and physical impotence and dependence by removing him from his role as a provider and protector. He may resent this loss of virility and productivity and become prone to moodiness and irritability. He may withdraw into a vegetative state in front of the television or behind the newspaper, exhibiting reluctance to engage in mutual activities out of passive aggression or self-pity. He may become depressed and forgetful. Sadly, death is often just around the corner for many of these men.

Basic Urges

(Autonomic Nervous System)

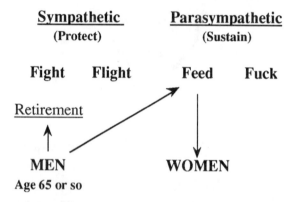

Sympathetic	**Parasympathetic**
(Protect)	(Sustain)

| Fight | Flight | Feed | Fuck |

Retirement

MEN   WOMEN

Age 65 or so

Countless men are mentally, socially, and vocationally castrated at age 65 due to the common policy of mandatory retirement. Since males derive much of their identity from their vocation (fight), and many of their other activities relate to work as well, a large number of retired men suffer identity crises and become anxious, irritable, and emotionally empty. Statistics reveal that a majority of men die within three years of being "put out to pasture." This indicates that retirement is a traumatic event, and that work and outside interests serve to keep men alive.

As a man ages and his power decreases, his partner may experience a temporary satisfaction from gaining more control (fight) in the relationship. But this is often soon overshadowed by the fact that he has become a burden or nuisance. While he was working she kept telling him to slow down, to spend more time at home (feed). Now that he does, she resents him for dragging his feet and not having the energy or motivation to get out and have fun. She sees this time in her life as an opportunity to catch up on things she has been missing, while he sees it as a time to enjoy doing nothing. He wants to forget about obligations and time schedules, to golf (a challenge) instead of spending his time in meaningful conversation or mutual activities.

A woman must realize her man's plight in this situation and avoid criticism and prodding. Such measures only cause further resentment. The man has just lost a part of his existence and may have to go through a mourning period before he is ready to face a new phase of his life.

Women adapt more easily to changes and cannot understand why a man becomes so unsettled and resistant. Although this frustrates a woman, she should try to be patient and flexible. If she does not allow her mate to find himself and, instead, takes over much of the things he should be doing for himself, he will become a weak, dependent person. Moreover, he may resent his plight and react by taking out his frustration on her.

We are all creatures of habit and tend to resist change. But change is how we experience new things and expand our minds. Resistance to change comes from a fear of the unknown, and is a part of our self-preservation instinct. Yet we sometimes carry our caution to an extreme by confining ourselves to a rut and going to great lengths to preserve sameness. As philosopher Alan Watts observed: "The greater part of human activity is designed to make permanent those experiences and joys which are only lovable because they are changing."

Although living a careful and conservative life may help us to avoid some pain, it opens the door to boredom and unhappiness. Learn to accept change—it's inevitable.

Basic Urges

(Autonomic Nervous System)

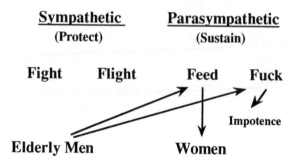

Most people assume that all elderly men are impotent. Yet a study by Duke University's Center for the Study of Aging and Human Development revealed that 54 percent of married individuals in their eighties and nineties still engage in sex. Another survey of men over 65 showed that 70 percent of those married still have sexual relations regularly. In view of these findings, post-coital withdrawal can still be an effective component of the geriatric male-female dynamic.

There is a common transition in most long-term male-female relationships that may be under nature's control. Studies have shown that during the first half of their lives, women trade sex for affection while men trade affection for sex. Later on, women begin to have sex for the pleasure and men have it for the affection. This signals a transposition of the emphases each gender places upon the basic urges.

Besides the strong levels of attraction and bonding provided by sex and passion, studies have shown that most relationships endure over the long haul largely because of *shared interests, similar values*, and *common goals*. So while the spark in the relationship is being maintained by passion, it is also important to develop common interests, values, and goals. This is the surest way to have a long and fulfilling relationship.

Loss of a loved one

A time will come when we must say good-by to someone we love, either through death, a move, or a divorce. Those of us left behind may experience sadness, anger, guilt, anxiety, and irritability. But when the parting is due to death, the more significant feelings fall into four categories, and we can experience any combination of them:

1. *Sorrow   for what we have lost and will miss.*
2. *Regret   for our shortcomings with them.*
3. *Relief   for the end of their suffering, and perhaps ours.*
4. *Hope   that someday we will be reunited.*

Over the years I have had to inform several of my patients that they had a terminal illness. The discovery of having bone cancer, lung cancer, a brain tumor, or another potentially-fatal disease comes as a severe blow. Such a discovery is tragic at any age, but especially when the victim is young. I will never forget the gut-wrenching experience of having to break the news to a young man who was just getting to the top of the world in his business and family life, including the recent arrival of a new baby daughter. This sobering experience, along with several similar ones, convinced me of the uncertainty and brevity of life. I now have a better appreciation of each new day and have resolved to live my life to the fullest and for the moment. I no longer live for tomorrow, for I know it may never come.

Many of the problems we encounter in life are traumatic and leave their scars. But the worst emotion a human being can experience is *loneliness*. No words can adequately describe the yearning and pain that follows the loss of someone we have loved. We come to understand that we have given them a part of us that will be theirs to keep for eternity. That is the "sweet sorrow" of parting.

To Be Or Not To Be

13

Relationships begin and end in subtle ways, and analysis of these subtleties provides information that can be used to strengthen a relationship.

Current statistics on divorce for various age groups reveal:

29% of those over age 50 have divorced
32% of those under age 30 have divorced
55% of those between age 35 and 50 have divorced

Clearly, our greatest danger zone for marital difficulty is between the ages of 35 and 50. Why would that be?

The answer appears to be *sex*.

Robert Sternberg and Sandi Wright of Yale University state: "The data we have collected indicate that the role of passion and sex *increases* in importance during the middle years of marriage." And according to Sue and Steven Simring, authors of *The Compatibility Quotient*, "The most predictive of divorce is a consistent lack of sexual desire in one of the partners." Often, the female is the one who loses her sexual appetite.

The Simrings further indicate that a role reversal of the female initiating sex more than the male often leads to unhappiness in the relationship. This results, again, from the male's need to be in control of the situation. Some men appreciate a woman who will take the initiative once in awhile. But if this becomes the rule instead of on occasion, a man may withdraw and become distant, or move on to another female who will allow him more control.

These findings leave little doubt that passion and sex largely determine the tone and longevity of a relationship. Passion and sex keep a couple bonded until the relationship can endure on companionship alone.

Risk is the fuel for passion. The fear of getting caught in an illicit affair or transcending social barriers to have sex with someone—such as a husband and his sister-in-law or a wife and her brother-in-law, or incest and rape, as extreme examples—escalates sexual desire and passion. This does not mean that you should always be suspicious when your mate is out of your sight, but it is wise to be on guard for such possibilities. Many women are shocked to find their mate involved with someone above suspicion. Your best insurance is to create enough intrigue in your relationship to keep your mate pursuing you instead of someone else. If you offer him enough challenge, mystery and passion, the chances of his looking outside the relationship to get his kicks will be reduced.

Intimacy blossoms in the light of respect and mutual interests. Extramarital relationships are more common among those who respect or admire each other, such as the doctor and his nurse, the boss and the secretary, the politician and his aide, the wife and her instructor, or the minister and the church secretary—or a member of the congregation. Sexual interest between a man and a woman flares up as quickly as thunder follows lightning. And when this interest is fueled by mutual respect and common ground, a hot affair may develop.

♥ ♥ ♥

Kathy and Don had been married twenty-six years. I had known them for some time, and had treated them over the years for an assortment of aches and pains and minor injuries. During a visit to my office one afternoon, Kathy broke into tears and finally told me she had just found out that Don was having an affair with his secretary.

Don owned a construction company and often worked well into the evening to catch up on his paperwork. Kathy used to work at the office with Don, but once the business could support a secretary, Kathy stayed home. She now spent much of her time baby-sitting for their daughter, Keri, who worked at a bank.

Keri learned about her father's affair before her mother did—informed by a co-worker who was at the right place at the wrong time and saw the secretary rubbing her foot up and down Don's leg during lunch at a local restaurant.

Keri took the news very hard and dreaded telling her mother. Although she knew her mother needed to know, she was afraid that her parents would split up. But when her anger became greater than her fear she asked her mother to lunch and spilled the beans. It was the same day Kathy had her appointment with me.

We started to talk about the unfortunate situation and agreed that she confront Don at once. Putting it off would only add to her agony and make matters worse. Don was not a violent man so I knew Kathy would be safe. I suggested that she ask Keri to leave her children at home in the care of their father—since exposing children to ancestors exceeding normal ranges of emotion would be unwise—and spend the night with her for moral support.

Kathy had to decide whether she would divorce Don. Many things had to be weighed, but rational thinking at a time like this is difficult. So I gave her some homework to facilitate sorting things out. Although a few experts have advised against using the Benjamin Franklin balance sheet to analyze a relationship, I do feel it can provide perspective in many cases. Kathy found it very helpful.

Relationship Balance Sheet

+ points	− points

I also asked Kathy to answer the following questions. These questions draw attention to the primary issues in a failing relationship and help to prevent a person from making a hasty decision based on emotion rather than reason.

Relationship Analysis

1. Am I putting more in than I'm getting out?

2. What is the minimum I must have to continue?

3. What would I be giving up if I terminated it?

4. Has he ever been the kind of person I would like for him to be?

5. Am I willing to give him a chance to earn my trust again? If so, what are the terms?

People under the influence of highly intoxicating emotions often take actions that are not in their best interest. Fortunately, Kathy agreed to be rational and objective. I suggested consulting with an attorney to find out what she could expect should she decide to divorce Don. In the meantime she was to list their assets, liquid and fixed, including Don's retirement savings, to assure that nothing would be shifted around or hidden from her. The attorney would want such a list should she go ahead with divorce proceedings.

To emphasize the seriousness of the situation to Don, I suggested having him move out of the house for the time being. Though she figured Don would simply move in with the secretary, Kathy agreed with my suggestion. The major benefit of the separation would be to discover how strong

the bond was between them, and give them some time to reflect on the life they had built together. An affair always
damages a relationship, but it can clear the air of stagnation
that has obscured the view of each other's needs.

Don didn't deny the charges and agreed to move out as
Kathy requested. To everyone's surprise he went to a motel
instead of his secretary's place. Don's greatest remorse came
from knowing that his relationship with Keri was damaged.
He hadn't intended to hurt anyone by his actions, but his basic urge for challenging sex had overridden his better judgment and caused him to do something he now deeply regret-
ted. Getting away with it had been half the drawing card. But
now that it was out in the open, Don's desire for the secretary dwindled as he looked at the consequences of continuing the liaison. He terminated the affair and fired the secretary, but had to go through an unlawful dismissal suit she
brought against him.

Kathy didn't divorce Don, but she filed a legal separation to protect herself financially. Eventually she dated Don
again, but also went out with other men just to see if Don
was truly the one she wanted. Don's courting gestures re-
sumed and he did nice things for Kathy that he hadn't done
in years.

Kathy played a little hard to get and let Don put forth
some real effort in his attempts to win her back. The two are
together again and Don is slowly regaining Kathy's trust.
Kathy attended one of my *Mating Game Seminars* and
learned about the effectiveness of post-coital withdrawal.
When Don gets a little moody and withdrawn, she steps
back and allows him to come to his senses. Before, she had
moved closer to him, only to drive him further away—
maybe even into the arms of his secretary. Now she knows
better. Instead of focusing on the past and feeling insecure,
Kathy is actively pursuing constructive interests that build
her self-confidence and personal value. This has made her

more attractive to Don.

Oddly enough, the force that pulls a couple apart often activates and strengthens the bonds that are holding them together—just like two magnets that have been separated. Though it took a traumatic experience to bring Don and Kathy to their senses and give them some perspective, they now have a better relationship.

Of course, not all "affairs" come to a happy ending. It takes substantial effort to preserve a marriage following infidelity, and not everyone is willing to make that commitment. But for those who are willing to invest the time and energy, broken relationships *can* be pieced back together.

Psychiatrist Kathleen Blindt Segraves of Case Western Reserve University in Cleveland states that men and women who engage in affairs most often site *boredom, revenge, the need for attention and understanding*, and *opportunity* as the reasons for straying. Although intercourse itself may not be mentioned as the culprit, men do blame sexual attraction and the need for variety more often than women do. When women have affairs, they tend to fall for a man who displays respect for them and showers them with attention.

Our attachment to someone depends less on who he is and more on what he provides. This is confirmed by the fact that our decision to perpetuate or terminate a relationship is usually based on what we are or are not getting from the other person. This means that we can worry less about who we are or how we look and concentrate on our behavior.

As we have learned, post-coital withdrawal can help to perpetuate a relationship by generating passion. Beyond that, according to William Lederer and Don Jackson, M.D., authors of *Mirages of Marriage*, there are four keys to a good relationship: *tolerance, respect, honesty*, and *a desire*

133

to stay together. Cultivating these traits will help you avoid the trauma of divorce.

To heal a sick relationship or maintain a healthy one, adhere to the following "Dos and Don'ts:"

DO	DON'T
Build your self-confidence	Criticize or demand
Develop your interests	Become his "mother"
Take responsibility for your own happiness	Bug him when he becomes distant and moody
Keep up your appearance, but accept your limitations	Do things for him he can readily do himself
Brag about your mate to others in his presence	Forget to tell him he is a good lover and provider
Use the bathroom privately	Pout or hold a grudge
Build desire by creating a little distance at times	Disclose everything about your past to your mate
Reward your mate for positive behavior	Assume your mate knows all your needs
Learn to be flexible	Let jealousy cripple you
Become better organized	Tolerate abuse

Funny as it may sound, the single greatest cause of divorce is marriage. But as long as joining with someone of the opposite sex continues to provide access to things we otherwise would not have, marriage will remain a popular institution.

Divorced women reentering the dating game face several challenges—especially when they have young children. The strain of juggling a career and child care can lead to burnout and depression. Combine this with difficulty finding a suitable partner and life may seem worthless.

Donna, 32, divorced, with two children ages eight and ten, was about to give up on men.

"Most of the men I date turn out to be jerks," she complains. "They seem normal at first by putting on a good front, but when things get a little serious, they pull away and behave unreasonably."

With two children from a previous marriage, Donna's chances of remarrying were diminished. Although she may be attractive and personable, most men shy away from committing to a woman who has small children—especially when the man has children of his own to support.

Donna felt uncomfortable and apprehensive during the initial phase of getting to know a man, since she knew she would soon have to drop the bomb about having two children. Although she did her best to appear confident and self-assured, Donna's experiences had conditioned her to be insecure and anxious each time she began a new relationship. Instead of becoming less anxious as the relationship progressed, she became more anxious, knowing that the relationship was getting closer to ending.

When a man senses insecurity in the woman he is pursuing he feels impending responsibility, which he may not be ready to assume. A woman in this situation has to be careful not to appear too dependent or focus on the future of the relationship. She should, instead, be appreciative of what the relationship offers at that point. This attitude will project an aura of indifference that attracts a man. As long as he is unsure of her commitment he remains in the pursuit. But once he captures her, the game is over and he withdraws— mission accomplished.

Judging by her previous experiences, Donna thought she would be better off living with a man for awhile before contemplating marriage. She would get to know him a little better, and, should things turn sour, she could exit the relationship with fewer hassles.

I suggested she look at the statistics:

According to a 1989 University of Wisconsin study, within 10 years after marriage, 38 percent of those who lived together before marriage separate compared to only 27 percent of those who didn't live together before marriage. Additionally, Jay Teachman of the University of Maryland reports that couples who cohabit are 50 percent more likely to break up than those who marry.

Donna also admitted a tendency to go to bed with a man early in the relationship. "Most men my age seem to expect that right away," she said. "They don't like going on dates and being seen in public, especially if they have recently divorced. They prefer going directly to their place—my place or a motel if he's married—having a few drinks and getting right down to it. They act like courting a woman the way they did when they were younger is a waste of time, even when they know it helps to build a strong relationship. But if I really like him, rather than lose him I give in."

Though Donna knew better, she couldn't hold out against a man's pressure to have sex right away. Her insecurity and desire to be intimate with someone caused her to go against her better judgment. The closeness of the moment did fulfill her need to be accepted and temporarily eased the pain of loneliness, but she was selling herself short, and she knew it. The only solution was simply for her to gather her strength and say "no." She did not have to get romantically reclined every time a man thought she should. In fact, holding the man at bay for awhile would permit the relationship to develop in several dimensions besides sex. This would provide better landing gear should the sexual component fail and force the relationship suddenly back to ground zero.

If a man packs up and leaves when denied what he wants—good riddance. Better at the beginning of the mating game instead of later when stronger bonds must be broken. If a man is so fickle that he leaves a woman over something minor, what would he do during the tough times when he is *really* needed?

In trying to perpetuate a relationship, Donna did everything she could to please the man. But when the sexual intrigue wore off and he began to feel smothered, the man fled, leaving Donna confused and depressed. Instead of putting her effort into building her self-confidence and improving her value as a person, she operated on the erroneous assumption that her ability to attract and keep a man was totally dependent upon what she did for him. Once she realized this was a fallacy, she was able to attract and subsequently marry a great guy who respects her and treats the children as his own. She even quit smoking, overeating, and taking tranquilizers. But most importantly, she learned to say "no" to the things that posed potential threat to her self-esteem and well-being.

Loyalties

Divided family loyalties have sent many relationships to divorce court. Since it is much easier to take on the responsibilities of your own parents than it is to care for your in-

137

laws, you must be careful not to let *your* loyalties interfere with your mate's ability to show care and concern to *his* parents. Balancing both families requires diplomacy and thoughtfulness. Once favoritism crops up, resentment soon blooms.

The hard fact is that when we accept a mate we automatically accept his family—parents, children, relatives, dogs, cats, etc. Though we may not particularly like associating with some of them we are obligated to do the best we can. Acts of thoughtfulness—a phone call, sending a card, a small gift—help erase feelings of neglect. Though everyone's life is busy, time out for a visit to pay our respects to our families earns us our share of respect in turn. It's a give-and-take world—quid pro quo—and we need to do our share of giving.

Raising children can also strain a marriage, especially during the teen-age years when the hormones are flowing. Children often show divided loyalties toward parents, parents often show favoritism toward children, and we have another vicious circle to contend with. But when we realize that nature is aiding and abetting this emotional turbulence to cut the apron strings, we can accept this as a natural process, instead of a curse. Though this phenomenon can create considerable stress and cause divorce, abuse, runaways, and suicides, it does make the survivors stronger adults.

Winnifred Cutler, Ph.D. explains it well: "As teen-agers head toward their independent years, their hormonal surges and purges and consequent disruptions help the family to accept this inevitable parting and even feel relief when it arrives."

Studies show that many of our social ills stem from incohesive family life. Since the negative influence of a family member is harmful to the well-being of the group, healing a family relationship can go a long way toward improving society in general. Getting along with all members of the family is part of practicing social ecology—it cleans up the environment.

When It's Not To Be

Sometimes we reach the end of our rope and realize that a relationship is over. We tried our best to make it work, but it didn't. Now we must gather up our strength and move on before life passes us by.

The pain associated with letting go stems from the bonds that have formed along the way. Although it has been commonly held that women are the sensitive gender and suffer more when relationships end, studies are showing that, in fact, it is the men who feel the most pain and loneliness.

While men are projected as being logical, rational, insensitive, and independent, they are, by nature, right-brain oriented—which makes them *more* sensitive and emotional. They have simply spent a lot of years perfecting their ability to repress their true nature and, therefore, appear sturdier than they really are. This, again, is a consequence of early man's competitive environment and the need to puff up and represent himself as a more formidable opponent than he actually is. Since nature's rewards go to the mighty, appearing weak and sensitive was not in his best interest.

So, while it may be difficult for some of you, have some compassion for the male of our species. Underneath his tough and unemotional exterior lies a warm, sensitive creature—like a turtle—who needs love and appreciation just as much as anyone, if not more. Although the weight of his shell slowed his progress through the years and camouflaged his true nature, it did serve him well. And, in spite of not needing it now, he has gotten used to it and feels insecure without it, since—like the turtle—getting a good look at the world requires sticking his neck out.

Some experts say that it is important to allow some time for mourning before moving on to another relationship, since a person may jump prematurely into a bad situation to relieve the acute pains of loneliness associated with the recent loss. But being too cautions may allow a potentially good partner to get away.

I believe that we must take our opportunities when they present themselves. Too many people postpone commitment thinking that they may find someone better by waiting. But they often don't, and live to regret it. As William Congreve said, *"Defer not till tomorrow to be wise: Tomorrow's sun to thee may never rise."*

So, do the best you can with the best that you can for as long as you can.

LIFE

14

$\mathcal{P}$eople have always pondered the meaning of life. Who am I? Why am I here? What do I want out of life? We have asked ourselves these questions ever since we became a reflective species. These questions are relevant to the mating game since we project our expectations of life onto our partners and hold them hostage to our personal belief systems. What we believe to be our mission in life greatly affects how we relate to our mate and other people.

With each major change in our roles, such as we have seen in the last 20 years, questions regarding who we are and what we want out of life take on an even greater significance. The current men's movement is a by-product of role-related anxiety and is an attempt by men to readdress the basic issues of their existence: to find out who they really are and what makes them truly happy.

Considering that we respond primarily to our basic urges, it is not surprising to see men using primitive methods in their attempts to find themselves, such as wilderness retreats that include dancing, drumming and other ritualistic activities. Our identity is deeply rooted in the past, and re-tracing our ancestors' footsteps gives us the perception of being closer to finding ourselves.

Unfortunately, the women's crusade that began a few years back became adulterated with an effort to emulate men. Instead of bettering their positions in life by exalting feminine traits (feed), scores of women vied to become more like men (fight). Consequently, many women now suffer from performance anxiety. They are expected to produce like a man and reproduce like a woman. Of course, slaying the dragon is difficult when your training manual was written for Cinderella and Sleeping Beauty.

Not surprisingly, some career women now long to be mothers and housewives. To keep one foot in each camp they launch business ventures that allow them to work out of their home. They have discovered that having it all is too big a price to pay. On the other hand, some full-time housewives envy career women, wishing they could get out of the house and do something productive. And so it goes: no one seems to be satisfied.

I would like to take this opportunity to give due recognition and praise to the women who have made valuable contributions to humankind as mothers and homemakers (feed/parasympathetic endeavors). Unfortunately, as women vie to become more like men, the global condition continues to shift toward the destructive, sympathetic (fight/flight) side, leaving us with less nurturers and Good Samaritans. Picking up a newspaper or turning on the television quickly confirms this. While some women may consider a life devoted to being a mother and/or homemaker menial and subservient, it actually improves the human condition by counterbalancing the suffering generated by the current sympathetic dominance.

So, if you're a mother or homemaker, be proud of it. Your lot in life is as valuable as your career-minded sister's.

Though life may seem a mystery and we search the world over trying to find a purpose for our existence, we all are here for the same three reasons:

1. **To Experience Life**
2. **To Make A Contribution**
3. **To Reproduce Ourselves**

To experience life simply means to engage in activities associated with expressing our urges, both basic and higher. It means to experience anger, fear, companionship, and passion; to be inquisitive, creative, playful, and spiritual; to feel pleasure, and pain; to laugh, to cry; to be accepted, and rejected; to gain, to lose; to give, and to take. Life is not full unless one experiences all of these elements. A combination of positive and negative experiences gives depth and perspective to an otherwise hollow existence. There would be little appreciation for the good and fine things in life without a cross to bear.

Life begins and ends with a struggle. Does it not follow that the interim would be likewise? We must face the fact that the essence of life *is* the struggle. It is the journey that counts and not the final destination. In spite of what we might prefer, life consists more of conflict and competition than of peace and parity. So, before we embark upon the high seas of life we need to get our ship together.

Men are biologically programmed to compete with men for power and women, and women are programmed to compete with women for beauty and men. We may be able to de-emphasize these traits to some degree, but it is unlikely that we will eliminate them. Success in our relationships with the opposite sex rests on our ability to accept and appreciate these differences.

To make a contribution simply means to give something back to life. If everyone took and no one gave, pretty soon there would be nothing left to take. True success in life isn't measured by what we *have*, it's measured by what we *give*. Having it all does not assure happiness and contentment.

Someone once asked Mr. Rockefeller how much money it would take to make him happy. His reply was, "Just a little bit more." Unlike Mr. Rockefeller it is time for us to ask ourselves "How much is enough?" and get back to basics.

Obviously, to perpetuate the species we must have children. Yet we also reproduce ourselves through being a good example for others to follow. This gives childless people an equal opportunity to make a valuable contribution to the future of the human race. If all of us strive to set a good example, we can eventually extract ourselves from the current predicament we are in as a species, and life will become a more appealing option.

There is no mystery to the popularity and power of various cults, crusades, and social movements. They feed upon a craving for acceptance and a sense of belonging—a craving that becomes acute in stressful times. By emphasizing and pursuing displacement activities instead of the more healthy methods of satisfying our true, basic, underlying urges, we have become an anxious and frustrated species. We do not relieve the "fire in the belly," and continue searching for something that will provide us with security and an inner peace. If we do not satisfy our basic urges, we experience an identity crisis—individually and collectively as a society.

There are two kinds of personal healing:

1. **Situational Healing**: Changes in circumstances: a new love, good fortune, etc.

2. **Attitudinal Healing**: Changing our minds about situations or circumstances that cannot be changed.

Much of the personal healing that occurs with involvement in a crusade or movement results merely from acceptance—becoming part of a *family*. This is what I call *situational healing*. When others accept us, our chances of survival increase due to having better access to things that satisfy our basic urges. We feel less threatened, our fight/flight urges are spared, and our feed/fuck urges are enhanced.

The power of acceptance plays a role in the male-female dynamic. The mere acquisition of a new mate (acceptance) can do more healing than years of counseling or psychotherapy. And although various medications can improve a person's disposition and outlook on life, a new or renewed love can do even better.

Acceptance provides an environment that is conducive to the expression of talent and creativity: the higher urges or higher self. Lack of acceptance activates the defensive mechanisms that suppress talent and creativity, prompting impersonation and imitation.

This reinforces my belief that there are only three things we are truly seeking in life, aside perhaps from reproducing ourselves:

Level 1 Acceptance
Level 2 Appreciation
Level 3 Admiration

These are the *Positive Triple "A"s*, in contrast to the *Negative Triple "A"s* of *anxiety, anger, and apathy.* Our greatest desire in life is to be accepted—by our parents, our mates, our children, our friends, our peers, and last, but not least, ourselves. The compelling need for acceptance has highly influenced our world and has given birth to countries, communes, religious sects, political parties, gangs, sports teams, social circles, family reunions, multi-level marketing schemes, support groups and 12-Step programs, to name but a few. Acceptance provides us with a sense of security and value. The desire to be accepted makes good actors—and sometimes fools—of us all.

Great healing can come from acceptance. Much of the benefit from professional counseling stems merely from the counselor's acceptance of the client. One study showed that people seeking professional help feel 30 percent better, on the average, simply from making the appointment. Knowing that someone is willing to accept us and hear us out is very therapeutic.

Yet our craving for acceptance renders us vulnerable to harmful associations and insincere displays of affection. Therapists, health care professionals, and others in positions of authority sometimes find it easy to take advantage of their clients. According to recent studies by Kenneth Pope, Ph.D., *Therapists who become sexually involved with their patients are more likely to be better educated and have higher professional status than their peers. They are also more likely to have undergone therapy themselves.* So beware! Credentials do not guarantee honesty and sincerity.

Finding a mate provides us with a sense of security and identification, and consummates our quest for acceptance. The trauma and insecurity associated with separation and divorce stems mostly from the rejection and loss of identification. Whether we admit it or not, we fret not so much over *who* we are losing but *what* we are losing.

Secondly, we wish to be *appreciated* for who we are and what we contribute, which gives us self-worth and bargaining power. And, finally, we want to be *admired* for our accomplishments, which gives us deep personal satisfaction and a strong sense of self-esteem. *We are not appreciated until we are accepted, and we are not admired until we are appreciated.* In turn, we do not appreciate someone until we accept him, and we do not admire him until we have learned to appreciate him.

I was acutely reminded of the universal need for acceptance, appreciation, and admiration as I was driving through a residential neighborhood not long ago and saw a five or six-year-old girl standing on the curb in front of her house holding up a coloring book so that those driving by could admire her work.

The sight brought tears to my eyes, with thoughts of parents who perhaps did not realize the effect their neglect was having upon their child. I pictured the father slumped in the recliner, beer in hand, eyes glued to the television, after having just told his daughter, "Go outside and play, I'm busy right now."

I pictured the mother in the kitchen on the phone with her girlfriend, catching up on the latest gossip, after also having told her daughter, "Not now, honey, I'm busy." Failing to get acceptance, appreciation, and admiration from her parents, the child turned to the streets instead.

How often does this occur across America every day? Not only does it occur in the parent-child interaction, but between couples as well. When we fail to obtain the *Positive Triple "A"s* from our mate, we begin to look outside the home for them: in our work, our leisure activities, or perhaps another person. Consequently, the relationship weakens and its value to us decreases. In order for any relationship to endure the test of time, mutual acceptance, appreciation, and admiration must be present.

	Level 1	**Acceptance**
	Level 2	**Appreciation**
+	**Level 3**	**Admiration**

Validation
(self-esteem/self-worth)

Our social ills stem not so much from the need for a better value system, but from the need for a better *validation* system. Validation is intimately connected to security, and when we fail to obtain adequate validation we become insecure and anxious. Increased anxiety (flight), in turn, generates imbalances in the *fight*, *feed*, and *fuck* urges, resulting in hostility, abuse, alcoholism, drug addiction, eating disorders, sexual disorders, obsession with fantasy and pornography, and on and on.

Validation is confirmation of our value. It's knowing that our contributions are needed and appreciated; that what we *do* counts and makes a difference. Unappreciated individuals become angry and resentful, taking out their frustration on everyone around them. Accumulate enough of these people and you will have a sick society.

Relationships are popular largely because they provide validation. They are a convenient avenue through which we can express our talents and abilities. It is important to remember that *relationships begin with acceptance, but they endure because of appreciation and admiration: validation and respect.*

The expectations men and women have of a relationship are different, and their needs reflect the contrast in their primary urges and modes of validation.

Women want:

To be in a secure, intimate relationship
To feel attractive and desirable
To be courted, respected and appreciated
To be a good wife and mother
To have a successful career

Men want:

To pursue a confident, elusive woman
To be a successful hero-figure
To have companionship / family
To be a good provider

A recent poll asked a number of married men what they would most like to change about their wives. The number one answer was: *"Her lack of self-confidence."* Although men are first attracted to young, beautiful women, they also prefer confident women. According to the research of psychologist Arlene Skolnick, marital satisfaction for both men and women is strongly tied to self-confidence.

Confidence is an attractive quality for both sexes. Since it is the opposite of anxiety, its allure comes from being the antidote for fear. Confidence, for both men and women, stems from being in control, which ultimately has its roots in **knowledge** and **experience**. *Knowledge plus experience equals power.* The more you know, the less you can be taken advantage of, and the more secure you will feel. Lack of knowledge and experience is the basis of a real or perceived loss of power or control, which causes anxiety.

Women are always curious to know the qualities men find most attractive. In working with thousands of men over the last 15 years, I have found them to be drawn to women who are:

Confident
Intelligent
Sensual / Sexy
Spontaneous
Humorous

To be more attractive a woman must exude confidence. This can be achieved by acting confident, pretending to be confident, or by truly acquiring sound knowledge and experience. It is, of course, best to have confidence based on real knowledge and expertise. Your partner may be disappointed should he discover that you are feigning confidence.

It is almost impossible to be knowledgeable in everything, so one must be somewhat selective in choosing areas in which to shine. As I've stated before, men are attracted to a woman who plays a little hard to get, which gives her an aura of confidence and leaves *him* a bit anxious. Confidence is a quality men admire and envy. And the presence of confidence is critical to the longevity of a male-female relationship.

A man likes to be in control. But when he is with a woman who is somewhat elusive he is not in total control, so he strives to gain it. With this in mind, a woman interested in validating her mate and perpetuating the courtship would be wise to let her mate have control over some things in the relationship—except for her. An ideal relationship is one in which the woman is in charge but the man thinks *he* is. In other words, if you *allow* someone to be in control, this means *you* are really the one in control. Yet many women refuse to see this point.

Ron Smothermon, M.D., author of *The Man/Woman Book: The Transformation of Love*, explains it this way:

> "Women do get their way, and one method of causing that is to have the man think he got it his way. A woman who wants her relationship with a man to work will do that. A woman who doesn't want her relationship with a man to work will simply get her way, or let him have his way and complain...In a powerful man/woman relationship, the woman is in charge. Her's is a natural

authority, derived out of nature and wisdom. She knows it and he knows it. She loves it and he loves it. Nothing else produces power."

A man's soul is in his work and ability to provide. It does not pay to attempt to take control of these two aspects of his life. Ironically, the harder a man works, the less his mate usually appreciates him, since work diverts his time and attention away from her. When he gets absorbed in his work, she takes it personally—she interprets this as his way of avoiding her, of neglecting her. But *he* perceives this as his way of showing more devotion to her and the relationship by being a better provider. No wonder men often comment at the end of a relationship, "I just don't understand it. I did all I could to see that she had everything, but it just wasn't enough."

Instead of using the time her mate is away from home to attend to her own needs and do something about improving herself, the insecure woman becomes critical and depressed, driving her mate even further away. She doesn't realize that by withdrawing herself and developing her own interests she causes her mate to move toward her.

Unfortunately, during anxious and stressful times we often feel compelled to vie for power instead of working in harmony. We may perceive threat in someone's actions or behavior and become defensive when he has not intended to hurt us. Anxiety distorts our sense of reality and ability to interpret correctly his intent and actions. This overreaction is destructive and deadly to lives and relationships.

The funny thing about power is that when we have it and no one challenges us for it we feel compelled to give it away. If, on the other hand, we feel challenged we will usually fight tooth and nail to gain more power just to make a point. A woman will have a stronger relationship with a man who enjoys doing things for her if she allows him to believe he's in control—just like during the courtship. If, instead, she starts criticizing him or vying for power, he will react to the resulting anxiety through *fight* (aggression) or *flight* (withdrawal), and both of them will end up frustrated and resentful.

Contrary to what some women may believe, men are actually very interested in pleasing women. But when the dynamic of the interaction becomes dysfunctional, the male's behavior turns sour and he becomes vindictive.

Despite the outcry of feminists, much of the power and control women have over men is due to sex. Men will always require women for sexual fulfillment, even if everything else between them fails. This is not a sexist statement. It's just plain fact. It's nature's way of assuring perpetuation of the species. And things seem to work best that way, provided everyone understands and respects the system.

It is foolish to think that we will have a better world by subordinating men to women in the work force, since biology has programmed the male to be the provider and validates him through a mate who needs and appreciates his accomplishments. Although women exercising authority over men will function in some instances, it is not likely to become the rule. Let's face it, females, by nature, will never exhibit the same consistency in the work force that males do, since they must take time off to have their babies. And, despite the publicity surrounding this issue, many corporations and businesses continue to view motherhood as a handicap to the competitive edge and manage to preserve the fraternal order of "The Good Ol' Boys." Consequently, it is more difficult for a woman to get to the top, and it always will be— until men start having babies!

LIBERTY

15

$\mathcal{F}$ear is the dragon, breathing fire on tranquility and causing widespread suffering. Fear (flight) is the greatest force that keeps us from achieving our goals and fulfilling our dreams. As Francis Bacon put it, *"Nothing is terrible except fear itself."*

Fear builds a wall to keep out success, happiness, and all the gifts life is so eager to impart. It stifles creativity, self-improvement, and accomplishment. It breeds insecurity, which, in turn, gives birth to anger and resentment. It prevents many relationships from forming and tears countless others apart. It causes physical and mental disease. It causes people to commit murder. And it is a short cut to suicide.

Considering the havoc and turmoil created by fear and anxiety, one of our most important missions in life is to overcome our fears. In the absence of fear and anxiety we feel powerful and in control. And being in control of our lives provides happiness and inner peace—qualities we all are striving to attain.

Ralph Waldo Emerson was not speaking lightly when he

said, "*Fear always springs from ignorance.*" Therefore, knowledge is our best ammunition against fear. Combining knowledge with experience eventually allows us to go where we previously feared to tread.

Studies on fear have shown that the fear of public speaking is number one. Why would people be more afraid of an audience than of heights, spiders, or even death? Considering that our greatest desire in life is to be accepted, and we multiply this desire by the number of people in an audience, it is no wonder we become anxious. To overcome the fear of speaking to a large number of people, look for acceptance and approval from only one person in the sea of faces. As long as you keep that in the back of your mind, you will be more relaxed and get your message across better, since you are addressing the group on an individual basis.

According to psychiatrist Frank Pittman, "*...intimate relationships have become our deepest source of terror.*" Since fear generates anxiety, and anxiety, in turn, causes us to behave abnormally, reducing or eliminating some of our fears improves our relationships with others. Identify five of your greatest fears and list three things you can do to overcome them. Start your list with your worst fear. Also, determine whether your fears are rational or irrational. In other words, if you fear being struck by lightning, and the odds of this are very remote, then the fear is irrational. If, on the other hand, you have a fear of going bankrupt, and your financial status is in dire straights, your fear is rational. By concentrating only on rational fears and formulating ways of overcoming them, anxiety levels will decrease and irrational fears will fade as well.

Should you have trouble coming up with ways to eliminate certain fears, check with your local bookstore for books on phobias and overcoming fear.

Fears   **Solutions**

1. _____   _____
_____
_____

2. _____   _____
_____
_____

3. _____   _____
_____
_____

4. _____   _____
_____
_____

5. _____   _____
_____
_____

Close evaluation of our fears reveals that we usually go out of our way to avoid them, which allows them to become even stronger. By acknowledging our fears we take the first step toward overcoming them. Then we must gradually allow ourselves to be exposed to the fearful situations in order to become conditioned to them. Extensive exposure to a stimulus—called "flooding"—eventually exhausts the nervous system and we pay less attention to it. It's like putting on clothes: you feel them at first, but after a while you don't realize you are wearing them.

Imagining something pleasurable when we are facing a fearful situation sometimes relieves anxiety. Instead of allowing our mind to concentrate on the fearful experience and become anxious we can focus on something that calms and comforts us, like laying on the beach, feeling the warm summer sun on our skin and the sand running through our fingers.

Others may benefit from adding a touch of humor to fear, such as imagining that the airplane in which they are riding is a strong, healthy albatross named Jonathan, with big goggles, who never fails to reach his destination safely. The bumps from air turbulence could be his maneuvers to dodge seagulls, or butterflies.

Sometimes we can displace a fear by imagining a situation in which there is an even greater consequence, such as a fiery car crash avoided by taking a plane instead. By concocting in our mind a scenario that poses a greater threat than the one we are facing, we can get through the actual experience with much less anxiety.

Our success in overcoming our fears is dependent upon our ability to change our attitude. Reality won't change, but we can change our perception of the situation. When we first learned to ride a bike we feared falling over and focused on every movement. But with practice we gained control, and our nervous system began performing the necessary actions and postural adjustments on a subconscious level. This freed up our conscious mind and allowed us to think about other things while we rode our bike, like what we were going to be asked on a test at school that day.

Since your mate's and children's anger and unreasonable behavior are stemming from fear, you can help them identify and dispel *their* irrational concerns. Knowing that anxiety stems from a real or perceived threat to one's existence—repressed or unsatisfied *feed* and/or *fuck* urges—makes locating the source of someone's fear a lot easier. Helping them gain knowledge and experience also builds their self-confidence and, ultimately, their respect for you.

A good way to assess a person's character—especially a potential mate—is to observe his reactions to stress. If he panics and exhibits irrational behavior he may be insecure, weak, and a poor candidate for a mate. If, on the other hand, he faces adversity head-on and looks for constructive ways to handle a given situation, he is probably a strong, adaptable person who is likely to be a good mate.

To identify your mate's or potential mate's greatest fears, and to get him to reflect on his life and the relationship, ask him to complete the *Ten-Question-naire* found on page 176. You may be surprised by some of his answers. Pay close attention to his greatest fears; they will tell you a lot about him.

The Pursuit Of Happiness

16

Everybody wants to be happy. We want to feel good about ourselves and be pleased with our lives and our relationships. But someone told us that happiness stems from a big event that transforms our life forever. This could not be further from the truth.

True happiness comes from the accumulation of a series of small satisfactions and pleasures, not some solitary, earth-shaking event. A study of lottery winners revealed that, approximately one year after their big win, happiness levels were about the same as someone who had suffered a serious illness. Although money *can* raise the standard of living, it doesn't buy happiness. Perhaps money's real value lies in allowing us to spread our misery over a wider range of acquired treasures.

True happiness is being yourself in your natural habitat, achieving satisfaction of your urges (desires, ambitions, goals, dreams). Abraham Sperling, Ph.D. of New York City College believes the ingredients for happiness are:

1. **Physical health**
2. **Satisfying work**
3. **Recreation and relaxation**
4. **A sense of belonging**
5. **A positive one-on-one relationship**
6. **Feeling secure and confident**

One of our most important assets in life is our health. Without good health, little else matters. Therefore, we must make health a priority and tend to it carefully. Health isn't nearly as hard to maintain as it is to regain. Once a serious illness strikes, great effort and a lot of money are required to recover. Sometimes death occurs.

Over the years, several of my happy, successful patients lost everything to a disabling or terminal illness. No words adequately describe this devastation. Ill people usually suffer moodiness and depression because of their decreased ability to pursue interests and satisfy urges. And, unfortunately, the financial strain of the illness adds to the anxiety and frustration.

The causes of many illnesses are yet to be identified, but proper diet, exercise, and stress management will always be the best prevention. Benjamin Franklin said it well: "An ounce of prevention is worth a pound of cure."

Doing enjoyable work that provides a sense of accomplishment is vital to happiness. Unrewarding jobs contribute to unhappy lives and relationships. Even though the job market is down and unemployment is up, with proper training and perseverance, most people can eventually get into some type of work they enjoy.

Considering the amount of stress we encounter today, proper rest and relaxation are essential. Periodic escapes from the regular routine prevent burnout and renew and refresh the body and soul. These times allow for quiet moments with a partner, to reflect, and to reprioritize things.

Fun and games are good ways to release built-up tension and improve attitudes. Just because you're grown up doesn't mean you can't play anymore. Adults are merely children who don't act like it—except for those who do.

Our aim in life is to be accepted, appreciated, and admired. This provides us with a sense of belonging and value. Our security is largely dependent upon acceptance, since belonging to a group provides increased protection and better access to the necessities of life. Studies have shown that individuals isolated from other people exhibit bizarre behavior and emotional problems, as well as suffer physically.

Our chances of reproducing ourselves and protecting our offspring diminish when society rejects us. Thus, our compulsion for acceptance may be bound up in our biology. The fact that most animal species also form packs or groups with a hierarchy of power supports this theory.

Having a positive one-on-one relationship is definitely good medicine. Studies have shown that people in a successful relationship are healthier, take better care of themselves, and produce healthier, happier children. If you are healthy, have a good job, receive help and support from your mate, have well-adjusted children, and have control over your life, you are more likely to be a secure, confident, and happy individual.

To keep your life under control and to assure the best chances of staying mentally and physically fit, make the following "Dos and Don'ts" a part of your lifestyle:

<u>**DO**</u>	<u>**DON'T**</u>
Develop a positive attitude	Gossip
Develop your interests	Expect too much of others
Choose positive friends to associate with	Over-indulge in fantasy and romance novels
Read self-help books and attend classes	Waste a lot of time on unproductive activities
Eliminate negative habits and addictions	Try to be the conscience of the world
Start forgiving others more	Let your life fall into a rut
Get proper rest & exercise	Take life too seriously
Be patient for positive changes to occur	Let disappointments spoil all the good in your life
Focus on helping others	Forget to set some goals
Develop a sense of humor & learn to laugh at yourself	Lose your head trying to save your body

Touch Me...Touch Me Not

17

The best way to demonstrate affection and acceptance is by touch. In a social situation we shake hands as a common method of showing respect and acceptance. This type of touch defuses potential aggression and provides a level of bonding.

Touching is an integral part of the mating game. It serves as a sign of acceptance—usually at the discretion of the female. It serves to build desire, and it provides bonding through sexual contact and climax.

Unfortunately, as a relationship ages the practice of non-sexual touching often declines. We call this *losing touch* with each other. Failing to keep in touch loosens the bonds in a relationship and the couple drifts apart.

The universal need for a loving touch is reflected in the titles and lyrics of countless songs: *"The Touch of Your Hand," "Touching me, Touching you," "The Love Touch,"* and many more. The strength of a relationship can be judged by the amount of mutual touching. While it may not be proper to hang all over each other in public, holding hands, putting an arm around a shoulder or through an arm are necessary expressions of affection. Touching is a warm and caring gesture and serves as a non-verbal method of conveying our love to someone. It is reaching out to share feelings, express emotions, and lend comfort.

Research has shown that touch is necessary for maintaining health. Infants and the elderly wither on the vine when not touched enough by other human beings. This is also true for those in the in-between years.

An Ohio University study of heart disease conducted in the 1970s fed high-cholesterol diets to rabbits. All rabbit groups began to show signs of cardiovascular disease except one, which oddly had about 60 percent fewer symptoms. This finding baffled the scientists, since nothing in the rabbits' physiology could be identified to explain their high tolerance to the toxic diet.

It was eventually discovered that the student in charge of this group of rabbits often took them out of their cage and cuddled and petted them for a few minutes before feeding them. The scientists began to wonder if simple cuddling could lead to a strong immune system. Repeat studies with other rabbits proved conclusively that it does. All things great and small thrive on a warm and caring touch.

Most women prefer non-sexual touching prior to engaging in sexual activity. This permits the feelings of acceptance, appreciation, and admiration to intensify to the point of arousal before moving on to intercourse. Men, on the other hand, prefer direct sexual contact expeditiously. Since a man's primary value to nature is procreation (fuck), direct sexual contact is the shortest route to fulfilling his potential.

Sexuality for a woman is more than *fuck*. Other parts of her anatomy are involved in the bearing and nursing of children, so she has a more comprehensive sexual nervous system. Her arousal is better accomplished by total-body stimulation rather than focusing on the sexual organs alone—except when she is highly aroused and moving toward climax. Men like non-sexual touching as well but usually prefer to dispense with the foreplay and get down to basics.

Most men will usually oblige a woman with adequate non-sexual touching once they are aware of this difference in the female sexual nervous system. But a man ignorant of this phenomenon often becomes resentful when his mate does not become aroused as quickly as he. This disparity causes problems in many relationships and has destroyed countless others. With proper education a man can learn to appreciate this difference and actually look forward to spending the time required to bring his mate to full arousal. The ecstasy associated with making love to a woman at this level of lubrication easily outweighs the fleeting pleasure of a self-serving "quickie."

I don't want to go into the vast inventory of specific sexual techniques, but there are a few things that have proven helpful for many couples.

1. A man needs to understand that a woman may not need sexual activity as often as he does, and he may have to supplement with masturbation. If his partner is understanding and loving, she might provide him with manual stimulation when he feels like having sex but she doesn't.

2. Most women require direct clitoral stimulation besides penetration to achieve orgasm. A woman can either do this herself, or she can train her partner to do so without saying a word by simply guiding his hand in a way that is pleasing. While in the missionary position a man can rest his weight on one elbow and roll enough to that side so that he can reach down with his free hand to do the stimulation. An up-and-down or rotary motion over the clitoris seems to work best, although some women prefer a side-to-side or other type of motion.

Vibrators or other devices may be used, but I don't recommend them as a substitute for something a partner can be taught to do manually. Much of the pleasure and gratification in the sexual experience comes from feeling and observing the responses to touch, so the less artificial means one uses the better.

According to hormone researcher Winnifred Cutler, Ph.D., author of *Love Cycles: The Science Of Intimacy,* weekly monogamous intercourse promotes fertility and physiological well-being in women. Cutler says that, "Regular sex seems to work in the body the way getting a weekly paycheck works in the household...Bonuses are always welcome, but only on top of the dependability of the regular paycheck...A woman's body seems to need the regularity of the seven-day 'receipt' of sexual contact..."

Cutler's findings further suggest that multiple partners are deleterious to a woman's health, and that regular sexual activity within the context of a monogamous relationship helps to counter the effects of aging. This may explain why some women who didn't especially enjoy sex in their younger years begin to do so as they get older. Their physiology probably knows what it needs to stay healthy and, consequently, raises the libido. This goes to show that milk is not the *only* thing that does a body good!

Even in long-term relationships men often fondle their mates—perhaps at inopportune times—as a way of showing affection and to feel accepted. A woman might acknowledge this display of affection with a reciprocal squeeze of her mate's genitals, realizing that he will usually take a rejection of his fondling personally. If his fondling is an attempt to initiate sex, a wise woman will keep in mind that a little resistance on her part will increase his desire for her.

Unfortunately, movies and videos create unrealistic expectations in men by depicting instantly-aroused females. Countering this "false advertising" with the truth eliminates much of the tension between the sexes and allows for more satisfying relationships. With knowledge comes understanding, with understanding comes patience, and with patience comes acceptance for the differences between us all.

Touch Me Not!

More respect has been built on saying "no" than on saying "yes," and a gentle resistance by the female helps to perpetuate a long-term relationship. But sending mixed messages while dating can lead to problems.

Much has been said about the mixed signals given off by women who initially say "no" to men but then finally give in and say "yes." The increase in rape—now estimated to be rising at a rate four times faster than crime in general—is often blamed on this paradox. But the increase in rape has more to do with the male's accumulated anxiety and repressed urges than the mixed signals given off by females. Women are unjustly blamed and asked to rectify the situation in a way that is contrary to their nature.

As discussed earlier, females are naturally resistant. This is nature's way of assuring quality control in reproduction. Males, by nature, are aggressive and forward. This assures an active and adequate supply of breeding potential: quantity. To ask women to avoid saying "no" before saying "yes" is unfair, since it causes them to violate the laws of nature. And asking men to repress their urge to pursue pits them against *their* biology. Besides, most women in successful relationships admit having said "no" before saying "yes," and that their mate was a bit of a pest during the courtship. Isn't this the mating game?

While vacationing at a Palm Springs resort, I witnessed the mating behavior of ducks. A mallard drake and hen frequented the same pool I did each day and occasionally slipped into the water for a drink and a swim. While laying in the sun beside the pool, half asleep, I watched the ducks and their rituals. Most of the time they engaged in feeding, meandering around the resort grounds picking up insects. The hen often took the lead, with the drake following a few feet behind. At one point she stopped feeding, stood with her head held high, and began bobbing her neck up and down in a rhythmic fashion—similar to shrugging shoulders in humans. The drake stopped feeding and intently watched the hen. Soon he was bobbing his head, too. A few quacks and squawks were exchanged in the process, and the drake moved toward the hen. She led him into the pool, swimming around in circles as he pursued her. Eventually he accelerated his paddling and caught up with her. Then, he bit the back of her neck and mounted her. The bite on the back of the neck temporarily paralyzed the hen and subdued her until the drake could get the job done.

This process had a striking similarity to human mating behavior in which the female is held strongly by the male. In rape, a man might hold a woman's throat to subdue her or keep her quiet during the act.

Since the chasing and physical activity associated with the duck's mating game seemed similar to that of humans, I wondered about the head bobbing. As I observed the mating behavior of several couples around the pool, no head bobbing occurred. But since males are visual-spatial in nature, I am convinced that a woman's body movements—flinging her hair, wiggling her hips, flashing her eyes, dancing about, hand gestures, or another behavior—serve to trigger men into action.

While this "sexual advertising" is obvious in ducks, it is more subtle in humans. Women inadvertently engage in certain behaviors that ultimately draw men into a sexual pursuit. In rape, knowing what those behaviors are could mean the difference between life and death—or at least avoiding a terrible experience that can result in a life-long struggle with post-traumatic stress. In many rape cases the attacker stalks the victim, much like the drake following the hen, waiting for the right set of circumstances to make his move. I am confident that research will eventually identify high-risk female behaviors and the most effective deterrents to unwelcomed male advances and acts of violence. Until then, a woman should take note of any gestures or behaviors that attract men. Although the ability to attract men is an asset, in certain situations it can be a liability.

The key to resolving the rape crisis, and most of our other social ills, is to relieve the underlying anxiety. Developing healthful outlets for pent up male urges and effective means to validate their manliness will do more good than asking females to stop wrestling men and, instead, take on Mother Nature. Nature is the more formidable opponent, and she ultimately wins—otherwise we would be immortal.

Males must first be made aware of their problem and, secondly, they must become responsible for their own recovery. Although passing laws against improper conduct may protect some women and serve as a deterrent for some men, merely placing sanctions on the problem will only serve to reinforce it. Rape is a compulsive act—a displacement activity resulting from the anxiety associated with the repression of an urge—and it must be treated as such.

Until men become better educated about rape, there are several things a woman can do to protect herself and minimize unwanted advances.

Predatory rape, in which the victim is attacked unawares, is a serious matter and entails special considerations, including specific physical maneuvers. Most communities around the country offer self-defense classes, and every woman should take advantage of one. With studies showing that the age of the victim does not matter to many rapists, all females are at risk.

In acquaintance rape—the form of rape a woman is most

likely to face—diplomacy and tact are paramount. When a relationship is to the point where a woman begins to feel undue pressure from the man, or she finds herself in a situation that promises uninvited advances, she must set the record straight in diplomatic but certain terms. Of course, if it is a relationship that she does not wish to continue, she should simply excuse herself and get away from the man as quickly as possible—before things get out of hand. If, however, she wants to be with him, she should know what to say to retain control of the situation. For example:

"Tom, I like you a lot, but I want you to know that I'm not ready for sex. If and when I am ready, you'll know it. Right now, I want to get to know you better, and I hope you want to do the same with me. I know you didn't just ask me out for sex, but I wanted to say this up front to avoid misleading you or hurting your feelings. Too many rape cases stem from simple misunderstandings, and I don't want that to happen to us."

These may be strong words for a woman to say—let alone a teen-ager or college student. But there is no better way for a female to handle the situation and prevent serious consequences. Some men are controlled by their sexual urges, and *vagueness or innuendos are not likely to deter them*. They must be confronted directly.

Most females, especially girls in their teen years, need assertiveness training. They must know what to say to a forceful man, since a lack of understanding or experience opens the door to rape. Failing to confront a sexual situation and allowing it to progress out of fear may lead to guilt and remorse—or legal proceedings—once a woman has had a chance to mull things over. Women are not responsible for rape, but they often are *guilty of not handling the prelude better*. Turning a man on and then telling him "no" is asking for trouble.

Drinking often facilitates rape. Alcohol lowers inhibitions and defenses, turning decent people into animals or easy victims. A woman should be wary in situations that involve heavy use of alcohol.

Obtaining professional help following a rape is a must. Look in the phone book under rape crisis centers, community services, or city or county agencies. Unfortunately, many offenders escape prosecution because their victims are afraid to face the legal battle and publicity. Still, offenders should be held accountable for their actions. Your efforts to see that a rapist is prosecuted may prevent someone else from becoming his victim.

Sexual Harassment

Sexual harassment has always been around. Numerous studies have found that males, universally, cajole females into having sex with them. Even animals display their specific brand of sexual harassment. But the question is: Where do we draw the line between acceptable and unacceptable behavior?

Since the tolerance levels to male mating behavior vary widely among females, it may be difficult to establish clear rules for proper conduct. What is disgusting to some women is acceptable—or tolerable—to others. Some women welcome suggestive comments and immodest touching at certain times of their lives—or during certain periods of a relationship—yet abhor it at other times. Further confusion is added by some "sexperts" who have gone as far as to recommend lewd remarks and the use of profanity during lovemaking as a way to spice up a relationship. The fact that this advice carries over into the workplace is confirmed by men who believe that female coworkers like to hear that kind of

171

talk.

When a woman is looking for a mate, or is attracted to a certain man, she may welcome heavy pursuit. But if she's not interested in him or the chase, minor gestures may be interpreted as harassment. Therefore, what is considered harassment is largely dependent upon the female's perception and tolerance. Since females have different tastes, it is difficult to set appropriate standards for all. We may have justice for all, but determining whether the crime fits the punishment is not an easy matter.

We have all heard of the happy couple who finally got together as a result of the male's persistent, and sometimes obnoxious, behavior. Although this kind of courtship may not be ideal, it has resulted in some successful unions. As some women change their attitude toward certain behaviors, some "assholes" become "gentleman," and vice versa.

The key to resolving the sexual-harassment issue is not merely to pass laws against it, but to *educate* men and women. A person unversed in matters of sexual innuendo is more likely to suffer anguish, and endure it longer, than someone who knows how to handle it properly. Unfortunately, some people put up with harassment out of fear of personal harm or vocational sanctions should they voice objection. This underscores the need for strict laws prohibiting the use of discrimination and violation of employment rights and privileges to retaliate for rejection of sexual advances. But enacting laws without concurrently changing attitudes simply results in congested courtrooms.

As public awareness on sexual harassment increases and laws stiffen to protect those who speak up, women will feel less anxious about blowing the whistle on offenders. Until then, a great many women will be intimidated by men who push things beyond the limits of good taste and tolerance.

A woman needs to confront an offender head-on. Ignoring the situation and waiting for it to improve only allows the matter to escalate. Speaking up early prevents hard feelings and resentment, and helps preserve a positive working environment.

I cannot stress enough the importance of saying the correct thing when it comes to handling harassment. A mere choice of words can spell success or disaster. Here are some simple, straightforward responses that clear the air at once:

If your boss keeps pestering you for a date, tell him, *"I really like my job and I'm trying to do it well, but I prefer not to go out with you."*

That should take care of the situation. Should he persist, follow up with, *"You are making me very uncomfortable. Before things get out of hand and I have to find a more effective way to resolve this matter, I'm asking you, politely, to keep our association strictly business. Agreed?"*

If that doesn't do the trick, a formal complaint should be filed with credible witnesses and/or substantiating evidence.

If you are offended by someone telling you his sex fantasies or repeating his worn-out string of bathroom jokes, tell him, *"I'm not interested in your stories. You have a problem that needs professional help, and I suggest you get some."*

When touched inappropriately, or oh-so-casually brushed up against, scream and say, *"Oh, I'm sorry! You really startled me."*

If you don't like being addressed as honey, love, darling or sweetheart, tell him simply, *"I prefer being addressed by my name. And I promise you, if you won't call me darlin', I won't call you darlin' either."*

It takes courage and fortitude to confront an offender,

but doing so builds self-confidence and maintains self-esteem. Though your relationship with someone may start out on the wrong foot, it can still end on the right one through tact and professionalism. Remember that much of your suffering in life will come from procrastination and denial of reality (avoidance).

As we confront our fears, our offenders, and our past more readily, admit our mistakes and shortcomings more openly, ask for forgiveness and forgive others more freely, we become a healthier, happier, more confident person. And if every man had a confident, happy, somewhat elusive and challenging mate to pursue at home, I believe that the level of sexual harassment and violence directed at women would drop substantially.

Men are certainly guilty of being insensitive to women's needs and often fail to put forth an equal share of effort to maintain the relationship. But let's face it, beating them over the head is not going to change them. Women can help most by playing the mating game with careful thought behind their actions and acknowledging human nature. By creating an environment that subtly motivates her mate to resume courting, a woman will improve her chances of having a warm and caring relationship.

Playing Ten-Questions

18

In working with thousands of men and women over the last 15 years, I have formulated ten questions that create awareness and provide insight into the problem areas of lives and relationships—a *Ten-Question-naire* for individuals and couples. These questions also can be asked of a potential mate to assess his capacity to be a good partner. Although it is impossible to detect every flaw in a person, a little extra time spent in objective evaluation can prevent you from making some big mistakes.

Since men tend to become defensive when their mates indicate that the relationship needs improving, I have structured the following questions in such a way that a man will not feel threatened by them nor regret his decision to comply with his mate's request to answer them. While some questions may not seem very important, believe me when I say that they are. Give each one careful consideration.

As you contemplate your life and current relationship, ask yourself the following questions:

The Ten-Question-naire

1. **What are your personal goals in life?**

2. **What are your family goals?**

3. **What would you change about yourself if you could?**

4. **What would you change about your mate?**

5. **What percentage of the time are you happy?**

6. **Do you enjoy your work? If not, what would you rather be doing?**

7. **Why did you marry your spouse? Would you do it again?**

8. **Do you feel you have changed since your courtship? If so, in what way?**

9. **Do you feel your mate has changed? If so, in what way?**

10. **What are your greatest fears?**

Many people do not set any significant personal goals. Instead, they slide through life, hoping that some magical force will provide them with what they want. But as you know, this rarely happens, and they become disenchanted with life and take out their frustration on those around them.

Personal goals are important to a relationship. They give some perspective and provide a means of evaluating whether the commitment is mutually beneficial. Personal goals also help to maintain some level of individual identity within a relationship.

We all have special things we would like to do or accomplish in our lifetime. Yet it's so easy to lose track of our dreams and get caught up in the crusade of helping a partner attain his. While there is nothing wrong with shelving your plans temporarily to help your partner do something that will ultimately benefit you or your children, you must be careful not to sell your birthright.

Life is short, often shorter than you may have planned, and you must make the best of what time you *do* have. If you are in a relationship that is a chronic drain on your time and energy, and does not move you any closer to the realization of your goals, you have three choices:

1. You can modify the relationship so that it can begin to give you a better return on your investment.

2. You can end it and move on, before life has passed you by.

3. You can do nothing and keep sacrificing your life for someone else.

If you are committed to preserving, yet improving, the relationship, your personal goals may have to be modified a bit to minimize conflict with your partner's goals—provided he has any. But you should not be expected to give up your dreams or postpone pursuing them for an unreasonable length of time. Discussing significant personal goals at the outset of the relationship will help to avoid confusion and resentment later on.

Another serious problem I see in most troubled relationships is a lack of goals for the family. Someone once said that, "Living a life without goals is like shooting without a target." Everything is hit and miss. But once a few goals have been set, a cause is born. This generates substantial positive energy and strengthens the bond between everyone involved. Mutual goals can include planning and saving for a vacation, a new house or car, a baby, college tuition, or starting a business. Hobbies or projects that allow everyone participating to make a significant and worthwhile contribution raise self-esteem and foster mutual respect.

Rallying around a common cause gives life and energy to a male-female relationship. Combining forces and working toward an end provides a source of appreciation and admiration. It's certainly a lot easier for a couple to commend each other's efforts when they are working toward the same goal.

Some individuals waste precious time fretting over personal features they cannot change. Identify things you would like to change about yourself, then decide if these changes are realistic. Wanting to become taller or shorter, obviously, is not realistic. Giving up smoking, losing weight, overcoming shyness, a limited education, a negative attitude, or low self-esteem are possible and rewarding efforts.

List the realistic things you would like to change about yourself, in order of priority, and begin looking for effective ways to bring about those changes. There is a ton of information available on practically every subject. If after learning what you can about a particular concern you cannot formulate a plan that will bring about the desired change, get help from someone—a trained professional if necessary. Making positive changes in yourself builds confidence, which will increase your attractiveness.

Privately, list things you would like to change about your partner. Then eliminate from this list anything that cannot be changed, such as his looks, height, etc. Communication skills, intimacy levels, grooming habits, parenting skills, sexual finesse, spending habits, attitude, and most behaviors can be modified to some degree with proper knowledge, a little effort, and patience.

Remember that people usually only change at the suggestion of someone they respect. If your mate has little respect for you, don't expect your suggestions for improvement to carry much weight. Work on building, or rebuilding, that respect, and you may be pleasantly surprised to find that he will automatically look for ways to improve himself.

Although I do believe everyone can improve themselves under the right circumstances, it is not a good idea to remain in a relationship with a violent individual. Trying to get him to change is often a futile effort and can put you and your children in extreme physical and emotional danger. It's just not worth taking the chance. Life is too short to spend it in misery waiting for an abusive partner to come to his senses.

Estimate the percentage of time you are happy. I usually recommend using the parameters of 75-100 percent, 50-75 percent, 25-50 percent, and 0-25 percent of the time. Most people think that something is wrong if they're not happy 100 percent of the time. In reality, no one is constantly happy. If you are happy more than 50 percent of the time, you are doing all right. If, on the other hand, you are happy less than 50 percent of the time, something needs to change in order to make your life a worthwhile experience. Of course, being happy 75 percent of the time and abused the other 25 percent does not mean that you are lucky and should be thankful for what you have. Such a life will still be destructive, and you need to get out of it.

Based on religious dogma, there are those who believe that the more one suffers in this life the better one's life will be in the hereafter. Whether this is true or not makes little difference. We all have the right to stake our claim to our share of contentment and happiness during our lifetime.

List what makes you happy. Identify the things you can change, cross out the things that you cannot change and *forget* them. It makes little sense to let things that cannot be changed ruin your life. Focus, instead, on items you *can* do something about. Seek out effective ways to make the desired changes; get help if you need it. And don't expect overnight results, since anything of value takes time to materialize. Though your life may be on the rocks, if you arrange them in the right order they can become stepping-stones to a new and better life.

Probably the most important thing to keep in mind is that it is in some of our darkest hours that we receive the greatest insight as to how we can escape from our predicaments. Be prepared for such revelations; look for them; they may be where you least expect them. By keeping an open mind the chances of a revelation getting through to you are greatly enhanced.

When you feel discouraged, look at those who have achieved success against great odds. You will soon see that excuses for failure are rarely legitimate. Instead of sitting around feeling sorry for themselves, these individuals channeled their anger and resentment into self-improvement efforts through an "I'll show you!" attitude. You can do the same. But be patient, success generally does not occur overnight. Remember that all your answers rest within you—let them rise to the surface.

If you don't enjoy your work, formulate a game plan to get a more enjoyable and rewarding job. Since much of our self-worth comes from our contribution to society, choose a career that is constructive rather than destructive to others or the environment. Doing something you enjoy and that benefits the earth and humankind makes it easier for you to obtain what you are looking for in life: acceptance, appreciation, and admiration.

The level of our disappointment in life is equal to the difference between our expectations and reality. If we constantly expect more than what reality can produce, we are likely to be very disappointed individuals. If, on the other hand, we don't expect too much more than what reality can deliver, life will be more satisfying and we will be a lot happier. This holds true for the mating game. If we expect a lot out of a relationship but have not done our part to nurture it, we are likely to consider it an unfulfilling relationship.

People often have false images and unrealistic expectations of their mates because of insincerity or deception, which leads to conflict. Set a good example for your mate to follow by being yourself. It is difficult to respect someone for who he is when he is always trying to be someone else.

Think back. Why did you fall in love with your mate?

—Would you do it again?

—If not, why not?

—What would need to change for you to consider him again as a partner for life?

—Is there anything you can do to bring about that change?

—*If so, do it! Now!*

Too many people suffer from the illusion that their life would be perfect if they just had a different mate, if only they had Mary's husband, or a millionaire, or Robert Redford, or...

Be fair in your appraisal of your mate and dwell on his positive features. It's easy to get caught up in the negative and fail to recognize the positive. We all have flaws and quirks that irritate others, and there are probably some things your mate would like to change about *you*. Understand that there is no perfect person out there waiting for you, though some may appear so from a distance. *We mold our partner by our own attitude and behavior*. So, focus on the positive aspects of your mate and your relationship, and do what you can to improve *your* attitude and behavior.

It's easy to identify changes in your mate since the courtship period.

But what about you?

How have you changed?

Have you become more critical, demanding, or impatient? Did your mate exhibit the same traits that now irritate you during the courtship and you chose to overlook them then?

Now that he is not actively courting you do you tend to focus on his flaws?

When the honeymoon is over and your mate stops doing all the little things that initially endeared him to you and made you feel attractive and appreciated—and compensated for his idiosyncrasies—you may make the mistake of focusing on his negative traits. With this action you are attempting to justify the disappointments and resentments you are harboring against him for not living up to the expectations generated by his initial courting. You also may resent the power he wields over certain aspects of the relationship. But reacting this way is destructive and pays no dividends. Concentrate, instead, on increasing your own value as a person, developing your talents, and building your self-esteem. This will entice your mate back into the mating game, compelling him to resume courting behavior.

Growing Apart

Married for twenty-four years, Cynthia and John, a couple in their late forties, had lost touch with each other. In the early years of their marriage they had shared many interests and common goals, including the struggle to make their flower shop a successful business. Now that the children were out of the house and in college, life had become routine and mundane.

Cynthia decided that it was time to do something before the growing apathy destroyed their marriage. She began attending one of the support groups I facilitated. Although John was somewhat resentful of her participation, especially when she had to leave the shop a little early one night a week to get to the session, he didn't stand in her way.

After avoiding active participation in the discussions for a few weeks, Cynthia finally opened up. She expressed her dismay over the insensitivity that most men—including her husband—exhibit toward women's needs. She felt frustrated. She wanted John to open up and be more sympathetic. When she became ill, for example, John did not care for her in a loving manner. He would oblige her requests for chicken soup, aspirin, a back rub, etc., but he always did so in a lackadaisical fashion. This attitude hurt Cynthia deeply. When John was ill she made him feel comfortable and cared for. Why didn't he feel compelled to reciprocate?

John was oblivious to the fact that they were in a rut. He believed that everything was hunky-dory, and that things were just fine the way they were. He didn't feel motivated to get off his duff to do some things that might put some spark back into the relationship. Cynthia was ready to develop some new interests and activities, but John was content with just going home every night and plopping down in front of the television.

Countless women have found themselves in Cynthia's

predicament: *married to a man oblivious to the need for growth and change.* These men have allowed their lives to dig so deeply into a rut the size of an army trench that they cannot see beyond the narrow path in front of them. Consequently, their peripheral vision and awareness of the needs of their mates significantly narrows. The solution is to catapult them out of the rut so they can see the real world again. This may require some effort and creativity, but it usually can be done.

People attending support groups have the uncanny ability to come up with wonderful solutions and advice for each other. But when it comes to heeding their own advice, rigor mortis sets in. Cynthia was offered about as many suggestions as there were participants in the group. She then had to narrow down her choices to a few things that fit her personality and confidence level.

As Cynthia and the group already knew from some of my presentations, most men do not respond to nagging. Men are project oriented; they usually like to be asked for advice. If a woman wants to get a man involved in something she will usually have much better luck playing upon these characteristics.

Close analysis of Cynthia's previous attempts to motivate John revealed that she had been *telling* him what she wanted. Instead of asking questions to pique John's interest and solicit his opinion she was defeating her purpose with statements like: "You never seem to want to do anything with me anymore." "What's the matter with you? All you ever want to do is sit and watch television."

Unfortunately, such an approach only closes a man off and makes him defensive and spiteful.

Cynthia desperately wanted to make John aware of her desire to improve the relationship. I suggested that she watch for a time when he was receptive and unoccupied, then ask him to complete the *Ten-Question-naire.*

Most men, when asked, not told, by their mate to complete the questionnaire, get the message that the relationship needs improvement. By allowing a man to come to his own conclusions he will feel compelled to put forth some effort to change his ways. The questions have been designed to create awareness, and to cause a person to take a good look at himself and to define or reaffirm his goals.

Apathy sets in when we lose sight of our purpose, become insensitive to the needs of others, and fail to recognize the subtle warning signs of physical and emotional atrophy. Short of a substantial physical or emotional trauma, or some type of spiritual awakening, these ten questions are the best way I know of to get a person to pause and take inventory. Getting someone to make changes in his life is like trying to get an animal to drink water. Forcing the issue causes the animal to resist, whether thirsty or not. But if the animal is simply made aware that the water is available, it will eventually partake on its own.

John took a few days to answer the questions. Without Cynthia looking over his shoulder he gave the questions some serious, uncensored thought. As he contemplated his answers he began to realize that he didn't have any significant goals. Maybe Cynthia was right, he *was* in a rut. Although pride made admission difficult, John did feel some remorse for becoming so insensitive to the person who loved him the most. He recognized that Cynthia was not happy, and that if he wanted to keep her, he was going to have to make some changes.

Cynthia was aware of male pride and how it prevents men from readily owning up to their mistakes—especially to a woman. She was compassionate enough to forgive John, provided he would at least make an effort to improve himself and make some changes in their relationship.

As Cynthia backed off and allowed John to move toward her, life became brighter. John began to pay more attention to her and asked for her opinion more often. He gave up some television time to take her out to dinner. He discussed the future with her and set some new goals. His talents and creativity, which had been dormant for some time, began to reappear. These changes delighted Cynthia and she found herself attracted to this "new" man.

Some couples communicate better through writing than talking. Eliminating the anxiety (flight) and defensiveness (fight) associated with face-to-face confrontation allows them to be more objective and rational. That's why the *Ten-Question-naire* works so well in situations that involve high resentment and low respect. It acts as a third party to facilitate communication, just as a counselor or therapist does. Also, it takes the focus away from the secondary issues and gets to the root of the problem.

Unconstrained writing can provide much release, even when the targeted person does not receive the missive. But communicating this way requires that words be chosen carefully so that no further offense is taken and the situation worsened. As long as a person is sincere and states her case in a loving fashion, most people will be moved to respond in kind.

Patience & Persuasion

There are times when a woman *must* make her case to get some satisfaction out of the relationship, or she has to offer constructive criticism to a partner who doesn't recognize a particular problem. She will have a much better chance of getting the desired response when she uses what I call *"The Art of Gentle Persuasion:"*

The Art Of Gentle Persuasion

1. Raise the other person's self-esteem
2. Subtly communicate your needs or desires
3. Make them aware of what you have in trade
4. Reward / reinforce their positive efforts

Put simply: *You will be liked and treated with more respect by those whom you have helped to feel good about themselves.* Before we can expect to affect positive changes in a person, or elicit positive responses to our requests, we have to have his respect. The best way to do this is to raise his self-esteem. Self-esteem is dependent upon acceptance, appreciation, and admiration. Therefore, we can raise someone's self-esteem by sincerely complimenting him, soliciting his advice, helping him achieve gratification of his urges, and avoiding criticism and other actions that unduly raise his anxiety levels.

Understanding the differences between men and women stops wasting your energies in unproductive areas and allows you to focus on specifics that will give you the most return for your efforts. *Men respond more to compliments regarding their ability to be a good provider and lover; women respond to compliments regarding their appearance and ability to be a good friend/homemaker/mother.*

Everyone likes and responds to compliments and favors. Kind words and deeds raise self-esteem and generate expressions of respect for the one with the gift for a bit of genuine flattery and deference. But you must be careful not to overdo your efforts to please a man or provide him too consistently with what he wants, since he will soon begin to take you for granted and become unappreciative. You must give, and then withhold for a bit to give him reason and room to move toward you.

Once you have adequately raised his self-esteem and respect for you, the time is right to begin subtly relaying *your* needs and desires. You may even find that by raising his self-esteem he is already looking for ways to please you. And, as long as you show him adequate appreciation for his efforts, he will keep it up. Remember that a human's greatest desire is to be *accepted*, *appreciated*, and *admired*. As long as you provide those needs to your mate, even in small amounts, he will be drawn to you.

Another virtue of importance is patience. When using the art of gentle persuasion, post-coital withdrawal, or any other method of eliciting positive behavior from people, learn to be patient. No two people operate in the same time frame or move along at the same pace in their life journey. Your partner may take a little longer to respond than you might expect. It's like planting a garden: we deposit seed in fertile ground, and then there is a gestation period before new life finally breaks through and becomes established. Unfortunately, many positive changes about to occur get plowed under by premature expressions of frustration or impatience.

All relationships experience periodic crescendos of tension that eventually erupt in some fashion. This is a natural occurrence, just like a volcano blowing off steam. This process gives perspective, helps to maintain individual identity and territory, releases tension, and fuels passion. To make attempts to repress this cycle—to avoid rocking the boat—is a mistake. Real boats rock.

This is also true in our relationships with our children. Periodic crescendos of tension, followed by release, facilitate the growth process and help children to become stronger adults. They gain experience in handling conflict. They learn to be cautious, and to protect themselves. They become more independent and better prepared to enter the hostile environment in which we all live.

They also learn to acknowledge and respect the feelings and rights of others. They respect us more by seeing our strength and willingness to stand up for what we believe in, though it sometimes brings us pain. They learn the art of conflict resolution and how to express emotions instead of repressing them. They see that two people can express their emotions to each other and the relationship endures. Of course, this holds true only when they see examples of *proper* handling of conflict or anxiety. When they see avoidance, denial, or repression instead, a vicious cycle begins, which gets passed on to each successive generation and becomes difficult to stop, leaving widespread destruction in its wake.

Private Matters

19

*P*robably the most valued quality of any relationship, business or personal, is *mutual respect*. It is the glue that holds the world together. It is also the magic ingredient that allows a couple to live together successfully. Isn't it strange that it can be easier for two people to live together who are *not* romantically involved than two people who supposedly love each other?

Clearly, love between two people does not assure that they can cohabit. A relationship will travel farther on respect than it will on love. And love will not keep your mate out of another woman's bed, but respect will.

The definition of respect is: *"willingness to show consideration or appreciation."* Therefore, much of the power of respect comes from appreciation—one of the *Positive Triple "A"s.*

There are two kinds of respect: 1. A willingness to put the welfare or desires of another before one's own; 2. Feeling compelled to do so out of fear or duress. In other words, either willingly out of altruism, or under duress due to the threat of harm or loss. Both forms of respect are active in the male-female dynamic.

A significant portion of the respect in a relationship comes from duress: a fear of loss, an element of dependency. When we receive benefits from associating with someone we usually avoid doing things that might offend them or cause them to cut us off. A woman can capitalize on this kind of respect when the altruistic form is absent. By temporarily making aspects of the relationship normally taken for granted less accessible a female can create a challenge that will draw her mate back into the mating game and cause him to court her again—provided he remains bonded to her.

A woman who maintains a little distance and privacy will build her mate's respect for her. Unfortunately, as a relationship ages, both partners often let down their guard and do things in front of each other that lower respect levels, such as nose blowing, spitting, passing gas, urinating, or defecating. Men are the worst offenders. One woman described being around her mate as "living in a gas chamber."

By using the bathroom in privacy a woman maintains a measure of decency and mystery, and avoids offending her mate. Most men are attracted to the scent of a woman's genital area, but they are turned off by odors associated with elimination, as are most women. Use an air deodorizer after relieving yourself. Being comfortable with one another does not mean performing bathroom chores in plain view with the door open and the window closed.

Don't forget your breath. Keep it fresh. Halitosis causes problems in many relationships. By maintaining good personal hygiene you are setting an example for your mate to follow. "Cleanliness is next to godliness," and godliness deserves respect.

Some things are best left alone, especially private matters. A woman does not have to divulge her entire past to her mate, including her past sexual experiences. I have yet to see these confessions prove beneficial to a relationship, except in cases of past sexual abuse or incest where the support of an understanding mate can prove to be invaluable. While honesty is a requisite for a healthy relationship, it does not necessarily mean full disclosure.

By preserving an aura of mystery a woman strengthens the bond to her mate and keeps him interested in her. Why divulge things that cannot be changed and take the chance of damaging the relationship? It's just not worth it. "Let the sleeping dog lie" applies so appropriately to past experiences. A woman can simply say that she wants to leave the past behind, and that each time she talks about it only brings it back to life. Most sensible men respect that and drop the subject. A male who continues to press the issue is only acting out of insecurity and will ultimately resent and eventually punish his partner in some way for her previous intimacies.

A man's desire to hear the erotic details of his partner's past sexual experiences arises from a morbid curiosity and the strangely stimulating effect of mixed emotions (fight + fuck)—comparable to watching someone else make love to his wife. "Telling all" will only serve to lower your partner's respect for you and weaken the relationship.

If a woman feels compelled to discuss sensitive details of her past with someone, she should do so with a professional counselor or therapist, not her mate or someone who might later divulge the details. Even though friends and loved ones should be our best confidants, they often are not. And when they violate our trust or use something we've said against us, our relationship with them is never the same.

The Winning Combination

20

The mating game is not as complicated as it may seem, and there are several constants one can anchor to when a relationship encounters rough seas. Men will always be committed to being a hero in the boardroom *and* the bedroom, and women will always be committed to being attractive and desirable. These characteristics are bound up in genetics and not likely to change very soon; therefore, it is best to acknowledge them and work with them to succeed in the mating game.

Women are beginning to stake *their* claim to the boardroom, but this is not their primary urge and may create conflict in their relationships. Besides economic necessity, most women work outside the home to obtain the appreciation and admiration they are not getting from their mates. Unfortunately, this search may lead to a new relationship with a man who, ironically, turns out to be just like the previous one.

To maximize her chances of mating and remaining with a successful male a woman must put forth effort to maximize and maintain her attractiveness. If she is also sexually intriguing, unpredictable, and spontaneous, her mating value will be even greater. For a man to maximize his chances of mating and remaining with an attractive, sexually intriguing female he must continue striving to be a hero in the boardroom (success/security), and he must make the female feel good about herself by reinforcing her self-image through adequate courting. Competition has and always will be a powerful component of the mating game.

Since finding a mate is not as difficult as keeping one, I won't spend much time discussing ways of finding the ideal partner. While some people may have good luck with dating services or personal ads, the results of an USA Today survey indicate the more common methods:

How People Met Their Mate

32% through friends and relatives
18% through school
17% through organized activity
15% through work
5% through church

Although these statistics don't show work to be the most promising way to find a mate, it does place a woman in proximity to more men. By getting a job among males a female can kill two birds with one stone: she can provide for herself while attracting a mate. Then, should she choose to have children, or has children but no mate and wishes to quit working to spend more time being a mother/homemaker, she can, perhaps, join forces with a suitable male who earns enough to allow her to stay home.

Unfortunately, the chances of building a lasting and sincere relationship diminish as a woman's level of success rises. Almost every male chief executive officer of all the

196

major American companies is married, while 54 percent of the female CEO's are divorced or have never married. In general, 52 percent of executive women are single or divorced as opposed to 4 percent of executive men. This lends credence to the adage, "You can't have your cake and eat it too." Or, as someone said, "You *can* have it all, just not all at once."

Though it may seem unfair and chauvinistic, many aspiring businesswomen will have trouble acquiring and keeping a mate because of the ego-deflating effect their careers have on most males. Nature has programmed men to be the providers and protectors, and mating with a woman who does not need male support fails to validate the man's sense of self. Just as a child's self-esteem is largely dependent upon his parents' expression of appreciation for his accomplishments, a man's self-esteem is contingent upon a mate who appreciates and relies upon his financial contribution.

Much has been said about the fragile male ego and its effect upon relationships. But biology is to blame, and biology is exempt from the laws of society—and deaf to the outcry of feminists. Trying to change men is a futile effort and a waste of valuable energy. Take the advice of Ron Smothermon, M.D.: *"Don't wait for human nature to change in your lifetime. You will grow old and never have any fun."*

Despite the effect female independence has on men, women should strive for a good education and training that will make them self-sufficient. If a woman loses a mate through divorce or death, it will be much less traumatic if she has the qualifications to earn a living. This is vital when she has young, dependent children.

My advice to women, including my two daughters, is to mate with a successful man, since poor people have just as much trouble with their relationships as do the rich. At least with a successful man a woman can enjoy a few of the finer things in life, and, should the relationship end, child support and/or alimony will be greater. Poor men can be good mates, but a woman has to decide what she wants out of life. Money may not buy happiness, but it sure provides comfort. And, besides, money is not the root of all evil. *Anxiety* is.

Many issues in a male-female relationship stem from unresolved sexual frustration. Although other aspects of a relationship besides the sexual component require care and attention, sex is a strong influence and subtly sets the tone of the entire interaction. In fact, resolving sexual difficulties often starts a domino effect on the other problem areas.

Catherine Johnson, Ph.D. recently interviewed one hundred couples whose marriages ranged in length from seven to fifty-five years. Johnson found that, "A large number of happy marriages, perhaps the majority of happy marriages, are founded in a deeply sexual love. Sexual connection permeates—frequently almost unnoticed—the friendship and working partnership that develops as time wears on."

When a man does not have an attractive, confident, elusive, woman to pursue he becomes moody, irritable, and his behavior turns unreasonable, which causes his mate to become anxious, irritable, and critical of his behavior. She then begins to question her attractiveness, becomes insecure and neurotic, and loses interest in sex—thereby completing the vicious circle.

Still, with post-coital withdrawal, increased confidence, and a different attitude, a woman can make the mating game rewarding and challenging again, eliciting better communication and more intimacy from the man in her life. With everyone concentrating on keeping and gaining access to their mate instead of someone new, the world will experience less chaos and strife. Sure, it's a game. But if you elect not to play you will be missing out on an an essential and rewarding part of life. As Pamela Redmond Satran said, "The only games I regret are the ones I wish I had played harder."

Perhaps somewhere long ago a female we might call Eve became insecure and decided to linger a little longer with her mate after lovemaking. Little did she realize that her need to linger would banish mankind from a Garden of Eden for thousands of years. From that point on man became unhappy and discontented, and embarked upon a prodigal journey that would take him far from his natural habitat, leaving in his path much destruction and waste.

From another perspective it could be said that man, underneath his complicated and multifaceted shell, is still a simple creature subtly motivated and directed by primitive urges. While he may think he is above such proclivities, he clearly is not. And for him to assume that these urges can be eliminated or ignored is pure foolishness. As he moved away from his early conditioning as a hunter-gatherer and began to live a more sedentary, rote lifestyle his natural tendencies were suppressed and repressed to an ever-increasing extent, and stimulation and exhilaration became ever-shrinking commodities. This ultimately resulted in extensive anxiety and great inner turmoil, paving the way for displacement activities to express and release the tension—just like animals in a zoo.

With attempts to eliminate or ignore these deeply-embedded drives failing, anxiety accumulated with each successive generation, and more drastic and elaborate displacement activities became necessary to provide relief. Unfortunately, the increased economic burden associated with gaining access to these sophisticated activities added further anxiety to the already boiling pot. Man entered a vicious cycle. He actually became addicted to his own anxiety and, ultimately, became a prisoner of himself. Hence, the dawn of the Thrill-Seeker Age, as well as exacerbation of our social diseases, such as alcoholism, drug addiction, sexual addiction, divorce, suicide, murder, rape, abuse, accidental death, phobias, nervous breakdowns and other mental disorders.

As stated by Patrick Carnes (*Out Of The Shadows*): "Risk, danger, and even violence are the ultimate escalators." To feel alive we stimulate ourselves artificially with chemicals, contrived situations, profanity, pornography, and loud music. We operate at such high speeds that we can't *see* the roses, let alone smell them. Entertainment has displaced self-improvement, and basic values have taken a back seat to accumulation strategies. Governments founded on the premise "to serve" now operate on the precept "to control." And the Golden Rule has become the Golden Ruse.

Despite the ambivalence and confusion that abounds, one thing is clear: *Our genetic heritage is more powerful than we realize.* And it is disheartening to think of the toll taken on lives and relationships through the years because of our ignorance and pure disregard for nature's deeply-ingrained format. Though our lives are complicated, we obviously feel "more at home" engaging in activities that closely resemble our primitive past.

When we cooperate instead of compete with human nature we find reprieve from our anxiety and experience true happiness. If we are to become more successful in our relationships with the opposite sex, as well as improve humanity in general, we must acknowledge these underlying forces and learn to use them effectively. While we cannot alter genetics on a short-term basis (thus far) we *can* minimize many of our problems by expressing our basic urges in safe, proper, and truly satisfying ways—instead of continually attempting to suppress or displace them. This work is an attempt to pave the way for such a renaissance.

I am optimistic that the world *can* get back on its feet. But since the male of our species is so confused and misdirected, the female is going to have to be the one to get up first!

Epilogue

Tired and weary, man left the path he was trodding and climbed the nearest mountain to rise above the turmoil for some reprieve. There on the mountaintop he looked upon himself in a new light and began to get a glimpse of the truth. Below, he could see the winding road he had traveled for so long. Suddenly, he realized he had been going the wrong way ever since he left home! With darkness falling upon the earth he decided to hurry back the way he had come while the path was still visible.

As he retraced his footsteps he was surprised to see how narrow the path had become, and he was thankful he had not tarried any longer. He felt ashamed of himself and the foolishness he had exhibited along the way. He now realized that happiness did not come from the world but from within himself. He was comforted by the discovery that he didn't have to earn his salvation, he had already been given it, and it was locked safely, deep within his soul. No matter how far he traveled, no matter what he did, he now knew that the only thing capable of separating him from his salvation was he himself.

As he neared home, he began to think of the truth he was going to reveal to his family and neighbors, and the changes it would make in their lives. He only hoped they would listen.

Guide To 12-Step Groups

Alcoholics Anonymous
Box 459
Grand Central Station
New York, N.Y. 10163
(212) 686-1100

Co-Dependents Anonymous
Box 33577
Phoenix, Az. 85067
(602) 277-7991

Gamblers Anonymous
Box 17173
Los Angeles, Ca. 93062
(213) 386-8789

Families Anonymous
Box 528
Van Nuys, Ca. 91408
(818) 989-7841

Overeater's Anonymous
Box 92870
Los Angeles, Ca. 90009
(213) 657-6252

Narcotics Anonymous
Box 9999
Van Nuys, Ca. 91409
(818) 780-3951

Cocaine Anonymous
Box 1367
Culver City, Ca. 90232
(213) 839-1141

Sexaholics Anonymous
Box 300
Simi Valley, Ca. 93062

Eating Disorder Resources

Food Addiction Hot Line: 1-800-USA-0088

Bulimia Anorexia Self-Help/Adaptation Support & Healing
1-800-762-3334   (24 hours)

National Association of Anorexia Nervosa and
Associated Disorders
Box 7
Highland Park, Il. 60035
(708) 831-3438

Anorexia Nervosa and Related Eating Disorders, Inc.
P.O. Box 5102
Eugene, Oregon. 97405
(503) 344-1144

Bulimia Anorexia Self-Help
P.O. Box 39903
St. Louis, Mo. 63139
1-800-762-3334

American Anorexia / Bulimia Association, Inc.
418 East 76th. St.
New York, N.Y. 10021
(212) 734-1114

Miscellaneous

Premenstrual Syndrome (PMS) Access
1-800-222-4PMS   (M-F, 9 a.m. - 5 p.m. CST)

National Sexually Transmitted Disease Hot Line
1-800-227-8922   (M-F, 8 a.m. - 11 p.m. EST)

National AIDS and HIV Information Service
(Centers For Disease Control)
1-800-342-AIDS   (24 hours)
1-800-344-SIDA   (Spanish, 8 a.m. - 2 a.m. daily)
1-800-AIDS-TTY (Hearing impaired, M-F, 10 a.m.-10 p.m.)

Aids Clinical Trials Information Service
1-800-TRIALS-A   (M-F, 9 a.m. - 7 p.m. EST)

Y-ME, National Organization for Breast Cancer
Information and Support
1-800-221-2141 (M-F, 9 a.m. - 5 p.m. CST)

Suggested Reading

Relationships

Enemies of Eros: how the sexual revolution is killing family, marriage, and sex and what we can do about it (Maggie Gallagher) Bonus Books, Inc.

Why Men Don't Get Enough Sex and Women Don't Get Enough Love (Kramer/Dunaway) Pocket Books.

Marriage Personalities (David Field) Harvest Home Publishers.

Intimate Play (William Betcher, M.D.) Viking Penguin, Inc.

We (Robert A. Johnson) Harper & Row.

Return To Romance (Michael Morgenstern) Ballantine Books.

Women Men Love, Women Men Leave (Cowan/Kinder) Clarkson N. Potter, Inc.

Getting The Love You Want (Harville Hendrix) Harper & Row.

Love The Way You Want It (Sternberg/Whitney) Bantam Books.

Faithful Attraction (Andrew M. Greeley) St. Martin's Press.

The Mirages of Marriage (Lederer/Jackson) Norton.

His Needs, Her Needs (W.F. Harley, Jr.) Fleming H. Revell Co.

Behavior

Personal Growth and Behavior ('89/'90) (various authors) Dushkin Publishing.

The Hare And The Tortoise (David P. Barash) Viking Penguin.

The Naked Ape (Desmond Morris) Del Publishing.

The Human Zoo   "   "

The Human Animal (Phil Donahue) Simon & Shuster.

Men

Why Men Are The Way They Are (Warren Farrell) McGraw-Hill.

What Every Woman Should Know About Men (Joyce Brothers) Ballantine.

He (Robert A. Johnson) Harper & Row.

Mantalk (Irma Kurtz) William Morrow.

The McGill Report on Male Intimacy (T. McGill) Holt Rinehart & Winston.

Self-understanding

Self-esteem (McKay/Fanning) New Harbinger Publications.

She (Robert A. Johnson) Harper & Row.

The Discovered Self (Earl D. Wilson) Intervarsity Press.

Man's Search For Himself (Rollo May) Del Publishing Co.

Personality Plus (Florence Littauer) Fleming H. Revell Co.

As a Man/Woman Thinketh (James Allen) DeVorss & Co.

Anxiety / Fear

Anxiety & Phobia Workbook (Bourne) New Harbinger Publications.
Life Without Fear (Wolpe) New Harbinger Publications.
The Wisdom Of Insecurity (Alan W. Watts) Pantheon Books.

Anger

When Anger Hurts (McKay/Rogers) New Harbinger Publications

Sexual Problems (Rape, Abuse)

Out Of The Shadows (Patrick Carnes) CompCare Publications.
The Courage To Heal Workbook (Laura Davis).
Free Of The Shadows (Adams/Fay) New Harbinger Publications.
Sexual Recovery (Gina Ogden) Health Care Communications.

Sex & Women's Health

Love Cycles: The Science Of Intimacy (Cutler) Villard Books.

Eating Disorders

The Deadly Diet (T. Sandbek) New Harbinger Publications.

Obsessive / Compulsives

When Once Is Not Enough (Steketee/White) New Harbinger Publications.

Divorce

Uncoupling (Diane Vaughn) Oxford University Press.
The Divorce Book New Harbinger Publications.

Finding A Mate

How To Find The Love Of Your Life (Dominitz) Prima Publishing Group.

Bibliography

Barash, D. *The Hare and the Tortoise*. New York: Viking Penguin, Inc., 1986.

Betcher, W. *Intimate Play: Creating Romance In Everyday Life*. New York: Viking Penguin Inc., 1987.

Brothers, J. *What Every Woman Should Know About Men*. New York: Balantine Books, 1981.

Carnes, P. *Out Of The Shadows: Understanding Sexual Addiction*. Minneapolis: CompCare Publications, 1983.

Cowan, C., Kinder, M. *Women Men Love, Women Men Leave*. New York: Clarkson N. Potter, Inc., 1987.

Cutler, W. *Love Cycles: The Science Of Intimacy*. New York: Villard Books, 1991.

De Angelis, B. *Sex Secrets About Men Women Should Know*. New York: Dell Publishing, 1990.

Delis, D. *The Passion Paradox*. New York: Bantam Books, 1990.

Farrell, W. *Why Men Are The Way They Are*. New York: McGraw-Hill, 1986.

Goldberg, H. *The New Male-Female Relationship*. New York: New American Library, 1983.

Greeley, A. *Faithful Attraction*. New York: Tom Doherty Associates, 1991.

Lederer, W., Jackson, D. *The Mirages of Marriage*. New York: W.W. Norton & Co., 1968.

Masters, W., Johnson, V., Kolodny, R. *Masters and Johnson on Sex and Human Loving*. Boston: Little, Brown and Company, 1986.

Naifeh, S., Smith, G.W. *Why Can't Men Open Up?* New York: Warner Books Inc., 1984.

Peplau, L., Rubin, Z., Hill, C. "The Sexual Balance of Power" *Psychology Today* November 1976.

Sandbek, T. *The Deadly Diet*. Oakland, CA: New Harbinger Publications, 1986.

Smothermon, R. *The Man/Woman Book: The Transformation of Love*. Complex Publications, 1985.

Sills, J. *A Fine Romance*. Los Angeles: Jeremy P. Tarcher, Inc., 1987.

Straus, M., Gelles, R., Steinmetz, S. *Behind Closed Doors: A Survey of Family Violence in America*. New York: Doubleday, 1980.

Van Hasselt, V. *Handbook of Family Violence*. New York: Plenum, 1988.

Watts, Alan W. *The Wisdom of Insecurity*. New York: Vintage Books, 1951.

Wolpe, J., Wolpe, D. *Life Without Fear*. Oakland: New Harbinger Publications, 1988.

Dr. Lyndon McGill, founder of the popular *Mating Game Seminars,* has worked with over 6,000 men and women in various stages of physical and emotional disarray since beginning his private chiropractic practice in Salem, Oregon in 1976. Dr. McGill has been a facilitator of various support groups for both men and women, and has lectured extensively on male-female communication, personal health and fitness, and stress management. Parties interested in sponsoring one of his work-shops can contact him at *The Mating Game Seminars,* P.O.Box 12037, Salem, Oregon 97309, or call (503) 362-6662.

Order additional copies of

What Every Woman Should Know
by
Dr. Lyndon McGill

Please send _____ copies of *The Mating Game* ($12.95 each plus $2.00 shipping and handling for each copy). Enclosed is my check or money order for $_____ (or complete credit card information below). Note: Advise if recipient is not purchaser.

Send to:

Name _____

Address _____

City _____ State _____ Zip _____

Visa / MasterCard #: _____
Expiration date: _____

Authorized Signature _____

Return this form to: **The Mating Game**
P.O. Box 12037
Salem, OR 97309

Phone orders: (503) 362-6662